Christmas messages and sermons suffer, perhaps more than most, from the dual threat of reductionism and platitudes. William Philip's short book takes the reader, with accuracy and deep devotion, from these wonderful songs of Scripture, to know, with new adoration, the Christ who was born. How much more fruitful Christian evangelism is when flowing from a deepening knowledge of Christ than from evangelistic clichés about the birth of Christ.
Peter Dickson, UCCF Regional Team Leader for Scotland

Familiar passages for many, but presented in a way that brings freshness, both in style and with new insights. The book is inspiring and informative, developing well the links between the Old Testament and New Testament. Written not just for those who have found their Christian faith but also for those who are still seeking and exploring. A great read for Advent!
Clare Hendry, Assistant Minister Grace Church, Muswell Hill, and Lecturer in Pastoral Theology

Christmas has always been a time for singing. In these rich devotions, William Philip unpacks the songs of those who first welcomed Christ into the world. Experience their joy as you hear the call to 'let every heart prepare him room'.

A wonderful exploration of the Bible's own 'Christmas carols'. Saints, sceptics, seekers and Scrooges will all find fuel here to warm the heart.
Jonty Rhodes, a church planter in Leeds and author of Raiding the Lost Ark *(IVP)*

William Philip, the cardiologist (or physician) who became a pastor, has written a book to make our hearts sing. He knows that Christmas is a time for music. It's a time when, right across the nation, people love to sing, and here are five songs from Dr Luke's Gospel that are in our Christmas DNA. But often we haven't pondered what we're singing. So why do we sing? Well, God is at work. John the Baptist is leaping for joy in his mother's womb. Can you believe it? An unborn child is expressing emotion. An old woman is having a baby. A virgin is pregnant by the Holy Spirit. I mean, what else can you do but sing?

Furthermore, a dumbstruck old priest realizes God is doing something extraordinary in his own life and lifetime, so Zechariah sings of a visitation from on high and a new dawn for the whole universe. This means, that with the birth of Jesus, a mass choir of angels breaks into song.

But Dr Philip also shows us that these songs from the Christmas hit parade are not a fantasy. He explains the truths at their heart. I'm so thankful for this fresh angle on the Christmas story. It has something striking for preachers, congregations and visitors alike.

Rico Tice, Senior Minister at All Souls, Langham Place, London, evangelist and author

William Philip

SONGS FOR A SAVIOUR'S BIRTH

Journey through Advent with Elizabeth, Mary, Zechariah, the Angels, Simeon and Anna

ivp

INTER-VARSITY PRESS
36 Causton Street, London SW1P 4ST, England
Email: ivp@ivpbooks.com
Website: www.ivpbooks.com

British Library Cataloguing-in-Publication Data
A catalogue record for this book is available from the British Library.

ISBN: 978–1–78359–447–4
eBook ISBN: 978–1–78359–452–8

Set in Dante 12/15pt

Typeset in Great Britain by CRB Associates, Potterhanworth, Lincolnshire
Printed in Great Britain by Ashford Colour Press Ltd, Gosport, Hampshire

*Inter-Varsity Press publishes Christian books that are true to the Bible and that
communicate the gospel, develop discipleship and strengthen the church for its
mission in the world.*

*IVP originated within the Inter-Varsity Fellowship, now the Universities and
Colleges Christian Fellowship, a student movement connecting Christian Unions in
universities and colleges throughout Great Britain, and a member movement of the
International Fellowship of Evangelical Students. Website: www.uccf.org.uk. That
historic association is maintained, and all senior IVP staff and committee members
subscribe to the UCCF Basis of Faith.*

For Rebecca, Joanna and Juliet,
who share this song of joy with me.

CONTENTS

INTRODUCTION

———————✦———————

The Glaswegian was a free newspaper that used to come through our door, rather sporadically, when the local delivery boy didn't just dump his whole pile down a nearby railway embankment. It really made little difference whether he did or not, since usually I put it straight in the waste-paper bin anyway! One Christmas, however, I was actually flicking through it (on the way to the bin). 'The Whole Tooth' was the front-page headline in bold: apparently, the big news in Glasgow was that a tooth had been found in a meal at a local Nando's restaurant. Strangely, I had missed that on the BBC News.

The rest of the copy was similarly banal, although one headline inside did catch my attention – 'What's your favourite festive song?' Five people in the street had been asked their views about their favourite Christmas song. The first went for Mariah Carey's 'All I Want for Christmas Is You': 'It's bright and cheery and it gets me in the mood,' she said. The next two both chose The Pogues' 'Fairytale of New York': 'It is such a rousing and happy song,' said one; 'Must be one of the most popular Christmas tunes,' said another. 'It really puts me in the festive mood and the mood for a good drink.' Oh dear. Then one man said, 'I'm not too keen on much of the recent stuff, but I love Handel's 'For unto Us a Child Is Born'. Three cheers for him, I thought to myself; Glasgow's history as a 'City of Culture' is not entirely a forgotten![1] Finally, I did chuckle at the retired doctor from Broomhill whose festive response was simply: 'I hate all the schmaltzy rubbish you get at this time of year.' There's always an Ebenezer Scrooge somewhere, isn't there?

That is a vox pop view on Christmas songs. But consider this: isn't it interesting that today, even in our secular world, people still do tend to think of Christmas as a time for music? It is always the time when music publishers rush to get a new album out because the Christmas market is the best of the whole year. You hear Christmas songs everywhere; they are played constantly in the shops and on the radio, and we probably play more music in our own houses at Christmas than at any other time of year. Even 'secular' people who rarely ever sing a hymn except perhaps at weddings or funerals will still often go to church to sing Christmas carols. People just seem to love singing at Christmas.

Perhaps that is because songs have been part of Christmas from the very beginning. Luke, in his Gospel, records for us five songs – songs of a rather different kind – that surround the birth of Jesus, the very first Christmas songs of all. Most of them are well known, and have been given many different renditions over the centuries, in both classical and more popular genres. You will see their titles on plenty of Christmas CD collections: Mary's song, the Magnificat; Zechariah's song, the Benedictus; the angels' song, the Gloria; and Simeon's song, the Nunc Dimittis. So from earliest times Christmas has rung to the sound of music, to the sound of song, and especially to the sound of praise and worship to God. It was George Campbell Morgan, the famous preacher of the early twentieth century, who said, 'When Jesus came into the world, poetry expressed itself, and music was reborn.'[2]

It could hardly be otherwise! If the One who was the focus of the praise of all history and all eternity was coming into the world, of course the world must break into song – what else could it do? Music and song are a necessary part of the proper human response to the work of God, and a natural way of responding when God is at work in the world and in our lives. It is as though we *need* song because music enables another dimension to our expression of response to God. Sometimes spoken words just aren't enough; we need the extra affirmation from our heart that music can help us convey. I guess that is why, whenever God's Holy Spirit has been at work in reviving power in the world, the result has always been an upsurge in song, with Christians both writing and singing songs. Think of the times of great evangelical revival in the eighteenth century that led to the wonderful hymns of Charles Wesley and others. Always God's saving work for his people leads to song from God's people.

By the way, it is always that way round – it is the work of God that leads to song. People sometimes get that confused, thinking that you can induce a work of God's revival and renewal by singing, and so endless and repetitive singing is used to try to create a spiritual experience. But of course that is back to front. It is when God is at work, and when his powerful message of salvation is being understood and being received by people, that they break forth in songs of joy. Salvation leads to song, not song to salvation.

This is exactly what we see in the opening pages of Luke's Gospel. Luke tells the story of Jesus' birth through the eyes of ordinary people who found their stories becoming inextricably bound up with the story of the long-awaited, promised Messiah, the Saviour of the world. When Jesus came into the midst of a dark world of waiting and longing, poetry expressed itself, music was reborn, and voices were raised in harmony to sing new songs – *Songs for a Saviour's Birth*.

1
JOY FOR THE HEARERS

The song of the heavily pregnant
LUKE 1:39–45

---✦---

[39] In those days Mary arose and went with haste into the hill country, to a town in Judah, [40] and she entered the house of Zechariah and greeted Elizabeth. [41] And when Elizabeth heard the greeting of Mary, the baby leaped in her womb. And Elizabeth was filled with the Holy Spirit, [42] and she exclaimed with a loud cry, 'Blessed are you among women, and blessed is the fruit of your womb! [43] And why is this granted to me that the mother of my Lord should come to me? [44] For behold, when the sound of your greeting came to my ears, the baby in my womb leaped for joy. [45] And blessed is she who believed that there would be a fulfilment of what was spoken to her from the Lord.'

---✦---

The very first song of Christmas belongs to Elizabeth, the elderly mother of John the Baptist, in her spontaneous expression of joy when she was visited by her cousin Mary. For some reason, Elizabeth's little song doesn't get a fancy Latin name like all the other ones. I'm not quite sure why, because, in fact, her song really is the first Benedictus.[1] While poor old Zechariah (who gets credited with the Benedictus) was still dumb, his wife Elizabeth was actually *singing* Benedictus – 'Blessed are you' (Luke 1:42). Her song starts just the same way as his, so I'm going to make a plea for Elizabeth to receive the credit for the first Benedictus, because at this stage her husband was still only capable of sign language!

Her song gets no Latin title, but nevertheless it is a very important song, with a very important message. I'm going to call it 'Joy for the hearers', the very first hearers, that is, of the coming birth of Jesus Christ. And it really is a song of great joy from the heavily pregnant Elizabeth. In fact, I suppose you could call it a song and *dance* routine, because it is not just Elizabeth who's involved, it is also John, her unborn child. It is John who quite literally 'kicks off' the whole thing (Luke 1:41). He leaps for joy within his mother's womb at the approach of Jesus in *his* mother's womb.

Joy in the womb

Let's start there: with John as he responds to the arrival of Mary to greet his mother, carrying as she did Jesus the incarnate Lord of glory in her womb. Luke 1:40 tells us that Mary entered the home of Zechariah and greeted Elizabeth, and as soon as the words were out of her mouth, we see an extraordinary, miraculous expression of joy. First of all, before anything else, Luke tells us plainly that there was *joy in the womb*: 'the baby leaped in her womb' (verse 41). Then Elizabeth explains it in her own words: 'The baby in my womb leaped *for joy*' (verse 44). So the first thing that Luke points us to is joy expressed by John, the intrauterine joy of a Spirit-filled, unborn child! John leaps for joy as he is filled with the Spirit, just as his mother Elizabeth was filled with the Holy Spirit, fulfilling what the angel had earlier told Zechariah: 'He will be filled with the Holy Spirit, even from his mother's womb'

(Luke 1:15). The very first hearer in Luke's Gospel, the very first believer, is in the womb, and he is dancing for joy at the presence of the Saviour when he too is still in the womb. Isn't that extraordinary?

You may find that hard to believe, but this is plainly what the text is telling us. Let me reassure you. Remember who is writing this – it is Luke the esteemed physician (Colossians 4:14). He is a doctor, so he is not entirely out of his field talking about intrauterine matters like this. He is no fool; he's a professional man who reads his medical journals. He isn't the type to be swayed by mumbo jumbo, but by evidence, and so I think we can trust his physician's judgment. (Being an ex-physician, I'm not sure if I'd have quite the same confidence if we were told that Luke were a surgeon! But even surgeons, I think, would have confidence in the investigative powers of Luke the physician.) The writer is a sober assessor of things medical, and he tells us plainly that John leaped for joy, filled with the Spirit, in his mother's womb.

It is evident from Luke's very careful historical writing, too, that he is not a man who indulges in speculation, but rather in careful evidence seeking. The first few verses of his book tell us that he has done meticulous research, carefully exploring every detail to pass on to us. He tells us he has examined everything all the way back to the very beginning of the story and has considered all the *eyewitness* testimony very closely indeed (1:2). He has done it purposefully and professionally this way to write an *orderly* account, and a *careful* account, so that his readers can be absolutely certain that all of it is true and verifiable (1:3–4). Luke goes out of his way to tell us just how scrupulous he has been, and when he reports what happened here, he is absolutely clear: John can have been no more than a six-month-old foetus[2] in the womb, and at the very moment Mary arrives bearing the baby Jesus, he leaps for joy. He rejoices in the presence of Jesus the Messiah!

Let me quote to you the late Professor Howard Marshall, surely one of the soberest scholars of the New Testament. He was one of my teachers at the Faculty of Divinity in the University of Aberdeen, and I can tell you he was not a man given to wild and unguarded expressions. His view is that 'a miraculous expression of the emotion of the unborn child is meant', and *not* 'that Elizabeth simply saw her own joy reflected in the unconscious movement of the child'.³ Just like his mother, John himself is filled with the Holy Spirit. This is joy in the womb, the joy of the first believer. More even than that, Luke is telling us that John was the first *evangelist*. That is what the angel had said to his father Zechariah, that this child would be 'filled with the Holy Spirit, even from his mother's womb. And he will turn many of the children of Israel to the Lord their God' (1:15–16). This is what John's Spirit-filled ministry was going to be about, even from his mother's womb, and now here it is actually happening! John, leaping for joy in the Holy Spirit, causes his mother to recognize the coming of the Saviour to her. That is Elizabeth's own confession in verse 44. She recognizes that the Lord himself has come, borne by Mary: 'For . . . when the sound of your greeting came to my ears, the baby in my womb leaped for joy.' Let's hear Howard Marshall again: 'She knew that Mary was to be the mother of the Messiah *by the joyous movements of her child in response to Mary's greeting.*'⁴ She understood, and she *believed*, because of John's intrauterine evangelistic dance. Isn't that extraordinary?

What on earth are we to make of all this? Well, quite simply that everyone – *everyone* – who is caught up in this story is caught up in something miraculous, because when God is at work, and when *his* story is unfolding in the world, amazing things happen. What Luke is telling us, all the way through his Gospel, but especially here in these opening chapters, is that God is a God who keeps his promises and he does so in the most amazing of ways. Remember what God's angel had said to Mary: 'Nothing will be impossible with God' (1:37). The God of the Bible is a God who makes promises, and we are to *believe* his promises. We are to *trust* his Word because his promises will always be fulfilled in their time. In the opening story of Luke 1, where we read about John's father Zechariah's encounter with the angel in the temple, Gabriel's censure is precisely because, unlike Elizabeth and Mary here, Zechariah did *not* believe the word that he brought from God. So he was rebuked, and struck dumb by Gabriel 'because [he] did not believe my words, which will be fulfilled in their time' (1:20).

This God always keeps his promises; he is always true to his word, and he does it in the most extraordinary and wonderful ways, even bringing a miraculous conception to an ageing couple, and even filling an unborn child with the Holy Spirit and making him dance in response to the Saviour. And, by the way, we should not miss some of the implications of this extraordinary encounter between Jesus and John when they are both still in the womb. John was perhaps twenty-two weeks old, little more than halfway through to full term of forty weeks gestation, and Jesus couldn't have been more than a tiny embryo, no more than a few weeks at the very most, something that many scientists today would simply call 'a ball of cells'. Yet his presence is already the human presence of God incarnate; already he is causing miraculous things to happen.

That is something we surely need to consider when we think about our attitude not only to abortion, but also to the whole complex area of embryo research, foetal stem-cell harvesting and other biotechnology which is often justified by medical researchers on the grounds that we are dealing with 'just a ball of cells'. Luke the physician sees things very differently indeed.

But here's another thing: John began to fulfil his destiny, the destiny of his life, even before his birth. Isn't that amazing? In

God's story, such wonderful things happen. Nor is this unique in the Bible story, for we read of other times where those in the womb are clearly already set apart by God for their life's work and destiny.[5] This should certainly make us think about our own children and our prayers for them, and God's hand on them, right from infancy, indeed from before infancy. God's beginnings with human beings transcend even our greatest understanding.

Of course, in one sense John the Baptist is unique, for he had a very particular place in the unfolding history of the coming of the kingdom of God. Yet in another sense he is not unique at all, because Elizabeth and Zechariah and all the others in Luke's story, including John, are also being deliberately set forth as examples for us, examples of true faith, a true response to God's saving revelation, and we are supposed to emulate them. Luke tells us right at the very beginning of his story that Zechariah and Elizabeth were 'righteous before God, walking blamelessly' before him (1:6), in other words, people of true biblical faith, whose faith, like that of all the great cloud of witnesses the Bible sets forth for us, we are to follow.[6] Yet Jesus himself tells us that even 'the least in the kingdom', that is, those who have trusted in the gospel of Christ, are *greater* even than John the Baptist (Luke 7:28), because we have the privilege of living in the day of salvation that was not as yet fulfilled in John's own lifetime. The gracious powers that surrounded John's parents, and even John's intrauterine existence, surround his people today all the more, for ours is a better hope resting on better promises, and the Saviour John prepared for has now accomplished everything 'once for all at the end of the ages' (Hebrews 9:26).[7] God knows his place, his plan, his purpose for every one of us who are his kingdom people, and for our children, even those still in the womb. We too are called to take God at his word, to trust his promises, and so to lead our own children in the way of the kingdom that God has promised in his gospel.

John's parents are an example to us in all this. At first, of course, Zechariah's faith faltered, and he had to be challenged and rebuked (as we will see later). But he took his rebuke, subsequently repented, trusted the Lord and recognized John's true destiny. In faith, he grasped God's covenant promises for his son and demonstrated his faith in action by insisting on naming him John according to the angel's command (1:63). We shouldn't miss this example of *faith*, of simply trusting God's word and acting on his command. Those who through faith are righteous before God, though they may falter, do not 'waver concerning the promise of God' to them and to their children (Romans 4:20).

Joy for the women

This brings us to the second thing to note about the circumstances of this song of joy for the first hearers. Joy in the womb is certainly experienced by John, but then Luke moves on to record the joy of the women, as expressed by Elizabeth in verses 41–45.

Immediately Elizabeth bursts into song; she exclaims 'with a loud cry' in response to the leaping of John in her womb, which in turn was in response to Mary's greeting. Nowadays we know so much about the intrauterine environment, with 3D ultrasound scans and other extraordinary technology. There is a trend for parents-to-be to read and play music and sing to their unborn children in order to influence their development. There may be something in this (who knows?), but clearly, what is going on here is something way beyond that. Surely Mary's greeting to Elizabeth in verse 41 couldn't have been more than just a few words. Maybe she blurted it out: 'I'm going to have a baby! An angel's been to see me.' Perhaps Zechariah, too, had managed to get across to Elizabeth via his writing tablet the whole content of his own experience with the angel, and she had been pondering it all throughout her pregnancy. Did Elizabeth suddenly put two and two together and understand it all?

We can't be sure, but however much Elizabeth may have understood, I cannot believe that Luke means us to think John in the womb consciously put two and two together and grasped it all intellectually. Surely not. I think it is much more straightforward to believe that Luke is recounting something simply miraculous and wonderful overtaking the lives of all of these ordinary folk. They don't yet grasp it all; nevertheless, the very presence of the Lord Jesus Christ in their midst changes everything for them. Elizabeth somehow understands that the mother of her Lord has come to her, and even John, unborn and in the womb, responds to the Lord whom he himself will be born to serve. There isn't complete understanding for any of them, but there is real joy, experienced truly and expressed vividly.

Often it is like that, too, in our own experience. Perhaps you have been going to church for some time, seeking after something, or maybe you even went to a Christianity Explored course. You now find yourself saying, 'Well, I don't understand it all completely yet. I can't quite articulate everything that I've come to see, but I do know that something miraculous has happened; something has changed, and the Lord has come into my life!' That has led you to an expression of real joy.

What Luke is showing us here is something like that. The women don't understand everything, but their joy is real because they understand enough to know that God has done a wonderful thing in their midst.

But notice the focus of their joy – I think this is fascinating. Both these women are newly pregnant. They have got so much in common, so much excitement about their shared condition. You would think, wouldn't you, that Elizabeth's song, her expression of joy, would be all about that: her baby? But no, it is not. Elizabeth does, of course, recognize with great gratitude what God had done for her in giving her a child (verse 25). But here in her little song her joy is focused in quite a different direction altogether; it is not joy about *her* child, but about *another* child, the Lord who has come to her, borne by his mother (verse 43). She shares in the joy of Mary's unborn son and she understands that he is to be her Lord.

Now, whether Zechariah had helped her to comprehend it all in his silent hours, and Elizabeth had understood it from him, we don't know, but her words in verse 43: 'Why is this granted to me that the mother of *my Lord* should come to me?' make clear that she did grasp what Mary's conception meant. She knows it means nothing less than that the Lord, the long-awaited Messiah, Israel's King, had come – and right into her own life too! The background to her expression is in Psalm 110, a great messianic psalm, and one that later in his Gospel Luke will record Jesus himself affirming as fulfilled in his coming.[8] It begins like this:

> The LORD [i.e. YHWH[9]] says to *my Lord*:
>   'Sit at my right hand,
> until I make your enemies your footstool.'

The psalmist David pictures the LORD God speaking to his Anointed One, his Messiah,[10] one whom the great King David himself calls 'my Lord', and Elizabeth understands that it is this King, the Lord, the Messiah, who has at last come – to her. Her joy is expressed in those terms, showing she has grasped that she is caught up in something momentous, something eternal. She understands that her own personal story has been inserted into God's ultimate plan and purpose for the whole world. And that is why Elizabeth's personal joy in her own domestic blessing, at having a son of her own, is totally overtaken by a much, much greater joy at what God is doing in *his* story, and the fact that she has been granted a place in that wonderful story.

It is something similar that always marks out people of real biblical faith. Their horizons are filled with much, much more than their personal circumstances, much more than just 'how God can fit into my life and bless me'. It is the other way round entirely in fact, for people of faith are taken up with the future that God is unfolding for the whole world, with what it means to be righteous before God, 'walking blamelessly' before him, as Luke tells us that these people were (1:6).

It is the same when we encounter Simeon in Luke chapter 2; we are told that he was 'righteous and devout, waiting for the consolation of Israel' (Luke 2:25), that is, taken up with God, his salvation and his great plan. Like Simeon, Zechariah and Elizabeth were real gospel people.

There's already a hint of this back in Luke 1:13. The angel says to Zechariah, 'Your prayer has been heard, and your wife Elizabeth will bear you a son.' It rather looks at first sight as though the prayer referred to is for a son, as if that has been Zechariah's constant prayer. But look more closely, and we see that this is obviously not the case. Clearly, having a son, or indeed any child at all, wasn't even on Zechariah's radar screen: 'For I am an old man, and my wife is advanced in years,' he says to the angel (1:18). That is why he disbelieves the whole thing. So a child is not what Zechariah has been praying constantly for and not what the angel means when he says his prayer has been heard. No, Zechariah's great longing has been that God's salvation would come to his people; his prayer has been for the consolation of Israel and the redemption of Jerusalem, just like the prayers of other faithful gospel characters like Simeon and Anna. These were real gospel prayers, for the coming of God into the world in saving power. And these are prayers that God always answers.[11]

So Elizabeth's great joy here, too, is not merely that God had come and answered prayer for her personal domestic situation, that 'God had come into her story'. But rather, as we saw earlier, her joy overflowed because she understood that she was being taken up into God's story. Her *real* joy was in understanding that what she and others had longed for God to do, he had now intimated he would do imminently in the birth of the Saviour.

That is not at all to minimize Elizabeth's joy at the birth of her own child. Verse 25 tells us explicitly that she rejoices that God has taken away her 'reproach among people', something she clearly felt deeply and painfully. And childlessness is a great sadness to many today, a real deprivation, very painful to bear, and sadly it is often met with considerable insensitivity even within the Christian church. In those days, however, and in that culture, it was even worse: not just a disappointment and a sadness, but a reproach, a disgrace. A woman's whole identity was based on having a child and an heir. But Elizabeth was a woman of faith and she knew that real joy, lasting joy, the joy that really matters, was never going to be accomplished just by having a child of her own, however natural a desire that might be. She knew that real and lasting joy was to be found in one place alone, in this child of Mary, in the promised seed, Christ the Lord who would be the Saviour of the world. That is why her joy is so immeasurable, why she bursts forth in song, filled with the Holy Spirit, when Mary comes to her: *because her Lord has come to her*. The source of true joy, eternal joy, had at last been revealed!

Once again, this is a powerful message for us today. There are so many things that we may long for, many joys that we greatly yearn for. For some, it could be just like Elizabeth's longing for a child. For others, it is the longing for a wife or husband with whom to have a home and a family, or for health, or a thousand other things besides – good things that bring joy, and it is not wrong to long for them. But true joy, although it is reflected in all of these things, is found ultimately only in the presence of the Lord Jesus Christ himself, in his coming to us, and our lives being drawn into his life and plan and purpose, just as Jesus came to Elizabeth when he was still in the womb of Mary. She understood even then that she had at last found the unfading, everlasting joy which could be found only in Jesus.

But how is that joy really found? What was it that brought both Elizabeth and Mary such great joy?

Joy in the Word

Joy is *experienced* first by John in the womb. It is *expressed* in song by the women, first by Elizabeth, and then in Mary's song too. But the joy they share, Luke tells us very plainly, is *explained* by the word, by the message of the Messiah to come. The road to joy for both women was belief and trust in the promise of God.

Elizabeth tells us in verse 45 that Mary believed that God's word would be fulfilled: 'Blessed is she who believed that there would be a fulfilment of what was spoken to her from the Lord.' Notice the contrast – was it conscious? – to Elizabeth's husband! Zechariah didn't believe that all God's words would be fulfilled, and that led him to misery, and to dumbness: his lips were closed. But Mary did believe, and it led her to joy and gladness, and her lips were opened in praise. 'Blessed is she who believed!' (verse 45). That could apply equally to Elizabeth herself just as to Mary, because she too believed God and welcomed the message of joy.

Do you see what Luke is telling us? The way to joy is *faith*: belief and trust that God's Word is true, that all his promises will be fulfilled. God keeps his promises of salvation, and Mary and Elizabeth trusted him and, in doing so, they found joy, real personal joy, as they discovered that they were being taken up in something wonderful, enormous, cosmic and eternal. They discovered the 'joy that is inexpressible and filled with glory' that belongs to a personal knowledge of the Saviour, Jesus Christ (1 Peter 1:8).

Mary illustrates one side of this life-changing faith and trust. When she heard God's word in the promise from the angel, she believed and said, 'I am the servant of the Lord; let it be to me according to your word' (1:38). She exemplifies *submission to God's truth*: she bowed her knee to God. That is one side of what the Bible means by faith: bowing the knee and submitting to God's plan and purpose for your life. But Elizabeth clearly exhibits another side of biblical faith: when she heard the good news, she received the message with great joy; *she rejoiced in God's truth*. That, too, is always a hallmark of genuine belief. Saving faith is a submission that rejoices in God and a rejoicing that submits to God's Word. Faith means gladly becoming a servant of God, gladly bowing the knee and saying, 'Lord, my life is yours.' It is also deeply and personally life-changing. These women were ordinary people, living ordinary quiet lives, but their personal stories became woven into God's story, a great story, *the* story of all eternity, and they became part of that story for ever. They found their own true destiny in God's unfolding story, all because they rejoiced in the promise of God, in the good news of Jesus Christ.

Joy to the world

The personal and life-changing nature of the message of Jesus has not changed since that first Christmas. People's lives today – ordinary people's like yours and mine – can be, and are, transformed for ever, just as Mary's and Elizabeth's were. That is why Luke painstakingly researched all this and wrote such a carefully constructed message. His story is not just about joy in the womb for John, and the joy found by these women, Elizabeth and Mary, who trusted in God's word of salvation.

Luke writes this for us also, and for all the world. His is a message of *joy to the world*, and it is just as wonderful today even though we are separated by some 2,000 years from the characters in this story.

If you are a Christian believer, then Elizabeth's experience is yours also. It is the same as hers and just as good – in fact, it is better than hers. The apostle Paul tells the Ephesian church that even former pagans who trust in the promise of God in the gospel of Jesus Christ are 'sealed with the promised Holy Spirit . . . to the praise of his glory' (Ephesians 1:13–14). John and Elizabeth were filled with the Spirit of God in the *presence* of Jesus Christ, but you also, when you believed the *promise* of Jesus Christ, have been filled with the Spirit of God. Your joy is the same, and so you also can sing with joy like Elizabeth and dance like John! You have everything that these women had. In fact, the New Testament says you have it *even better*, because everything that she believed that God *would* fulfil through the birth of this baby Jesus, God *did* fulfil and has accomplished for ever, and we have the proof and the certainty of it in Jesus Christ's resurrection from the dead. We have *more* evidence, *more* solid buttressing for our faith than even Elizabeth and Mary had at this stage, eyewitnesses of such extraordinary events though they were. There has been a fulfilment of everything that God promised in Jesus Christ, risen and ascended to glory, and that is why there is joy for the world.

This is the real message of the coming of Jesus that we celebrate at Christmas. It is a message of joy for us also, which is why we sing,

> Good Christian men, rejoice
> with heart and soul and voice![12]

The joy of Christmas is for every single Christian believer. That is what Jesus came to bring to us. The saving mercy promised by John the Baptist has indeed become ours through Jesus Christ.

Sometimes we read these wonderful stories and are tempted to think rather romantically, 'Wouldn't it be wonderful if we had been John or Elizabeth, or if we had been there and seen these wonderful things!' Well, yes, in one sense of course it would, but the glory of the gospel is that it is even more wonderful for everyone who is in the kingdom of God today. We have a greater experience of joy than all these, greater even than that of John the Baptist, the forerunner who announced the Messiah's presence at last. Jesus said that because of John's uniquely privileged prophetic ministry, 'none is greater than John . . .' Nevertheless, because God keeps his promises, and because he has fulfilled everything he had spoken, Jesus goes on to say, 'Yet the one who is least in the kingdom of God is greater than he' (Luke 7:28).

Of course, it's possible that you are not a convinced Christian, a persuaded believer in God's promise. What about you then? Well, if Luke's message really is 'joy to the world', it must mean that there can be joy for you also, if only you will receive the message and so join the joy. There is still *joy for the hearers*, for all who will hear the message and believe and trust with all their heart and express that trust, as Elizabeth did, in joyful worship and praise. The Christmas message still comes to everyone today, in the message of the gospel of Jesus Christ.

> For the Scripture says, '*Everyone* who believes in him will not be put to shame.' For there is no distinction between Jew and Greek; the same Lord is Lord of all, bestowing his riches on *all* who call on him. For '*everyone* who calls on the name of the Lord will be saved.'
> (ROMANS 10:11–13)

You really can't miss that promise: *everyone who calls on the name of the Lord will be saved*. That is our God's way: he is the God of grace and gratuitous mercy.

The way to joy is through faith, and the way to faith is by hearing the word of promise. Jesus came to Elizabeth, and she found everlasting joy, joy in the Lord who fulfilled every one of his promises that he had made to her and to the world. He comes to us today, and joy still comes just the same way, through faith, which likewise still comes by hearing God's words of promise.

So Luke wrote his Gospel to us, recording this song of joy, so that, like the first hearers, we too would sing for joy. He wrote his Gospel not just that we should marvel at what happened to John, and Elizabeth and Mary, and the others surrounding the crib, but that we too would join the joy. Luke 1:45 could be paraphrased thus:

> Blessed is everyone, then and now, who believes that there will be a fulfilment of what is spoken by the Lord!

The message of Christmas today, whether you are a Christian believer or haven't yet put your trust in Jesus Christ, is the same: join the joy! Join the joy of all true hearers, and share it too, as you, like Elizabeth, express to others the joy that is in your heart because of the coming of the Saviour.

2
JOY FOR THE HUMBLE

The song of a humble peasant
LUKE 1:46–55

———✦———

⁴⁶And Mary said,

'My soul magnifies the Lord,
   ⁴⁷and my spirit rejoices in God my Saviour,
⁴⁸for he has looked on the humble estate of his
      servant.
   For behold, from now on all generations will call
      me blessed;
⁴⁹for he who is mighty has done great things for me,
   and holy is his name.
⁵⁰And his mercy is for those who fear him
   from generation to generation.
⁵¹He has shown strength with his arm;
   he has scattered the proud in the thoughts of
      their hearts;
⁵²he has brought down the mighty from their
      thrones
   and exalted those of humble estate;
⁵³he has filled the hungry with good things,
   and the rich he has sent away empty.

> [54]He has helped his servant Israel,
>   in remembrance of his mercy,
> [55]as he spoke to our fathers,
>   to Abraham and to his offspring for ever.'

———————✦———————

Luke 1:46–55 contains the words of the second of the original Christmas songs Luke records for us, the famous Magnificat which has been set to music by many different composers over the centuries.[1] Magnificat just means 'magnify', which is the first word of the song in Latin (the language of the medieval church, and hence of much choral church music).

In declaring 'My soul magnifies the Lord', Mary is giving voice to words which the Holy Spirit of God inspired in her as she responded with faith to the extraordinary promise from God about his coming as Saviour. She was to bear a son who would be God's chosen King, to reign over a kingdom that has no end, because he would be God himself born in the flesh.[2] We are told that Mary 'believed there would be a fulfilment of what was spoken to her from the Lord',[3] and so she adds her voice to Elizabeth's in singing a song of joy to God.

Now, no doubt each of these women was full of emotion about what had happened to them, both the extraordinary events they had shared in, and also their approaching motherhood. As we saw earlier, Elizabeth would have been overjoyed by the totally unexpected end to her long barren years, but for Mary things were very different. She must have been very young, and her pregnancy was certainly an equally unexpected great shock. But, having digested the news, these two expectant mothers had plenty to talk about together, plenty to sing about.

But the strange thing is, as I'm sure you'll have noticed, Mary's song isn't actually about a baby at all! It is certainly not the kind of song you would hear playing in Mothercare stores. No, in fact it is a very theological song (a song about *God*). But it is not simply a song thanking God for what has been happening in her own life, and her approaching motherhood. It has far bigger horizons in view. Mary seems to see this divine intervention into her own life as something that affects not just her, but the whole of the universe, for ever.

One of the things that those familiar with the Bible often recognize is that Mary's song echoes the song of another woman we read of in the Old Testament, hundreds of years earlier, that of Hannah the mother of Samuel (1 Samuel 2:1–10). She too sang of a child God had granted her, but she likewise saw in her child's birth a far greater significance than merely personal joy at having a baby. Her child would usher in a new era for God's people, Israel, and indeed, he would prepare the way for a king, King David, who would rule the land, bringing peace and glory to his kingdom. Mary's song echoes that earlier song of promise and hope, but does so in a far greater way, and with a far greater and wider significance, for at last, in the coming of *this* king, God's saving purposes would bring peace and glory to the whole earth.

This is why Mary's song isn't about her own pregnancy or about parenthood, wonderful as they are. No, instead Mary sings all about the *significance* of the birth that is to come: a birth unlike any other there ever has been, or ever will be. Mary understood the message that this first Christmas would bring to the whole world. In the coming of Jesus, God was speaking, telling her – and the whole world – that he is the God who saves. *God himself was coming to save his people.* This is what Mary is singing about, and in so doing, she explains to us just how God's plan of salvation comes to its fullness in Jesus Christ.

History explained by God

Let's begin at the end of Mary's song (verses 54–55). Mary tells us here that in the coming of Jesus Christ, all history is at last being explained by God. In Jesus comes the meaning that banishes the mystery about the world as we know it today, and have known it throughout all its history.

> He has helped his servant Israel,
>> in remembrance of his mercy,
> as he spoke to our fathers,
>> to Abraham and to his offspring for ever.

Mary is looking right back throughout history and seeing that in Jesus' coming God has at last kept all his promises to human beings from the very beginning. He has remembered his words of mercy which go right back to Abraham, to the very start of Israel's history as a people, and therefore Jesus is the explanation, at last, of everything the whole world has been waiting for.

Our world and all its history is something of a mystery to us. It is so hard to fathom, with its shifts in geopolitics, its changing powers and its astonishing technological progress. Yet in another way, the world seems to change very little. I expect that in the Middle East today some places in the hill country of Galilee and Nazareth are not so very different from what they were 2,000 years ago, and certainly not for a peasant girl living on the West Bank of the River Jordan. In those days, too, it was occupied territory, although then it was the Jews who were occupied by the hated Romans, and many in Israel lived with the mystery of a God who seemed to be totally absent, or at least very distant.

God's people, Israel, had many enemies; her history had been very fractured, involving centuries of subjugation and even exile from the Land of Promise in faraway Babylon. The Israelites had returned, with great expectations, it is true. The prophets had spoken of a wonderful future and a change in the whole world. Yet centuries had passed, and year rolled on to year, but little or nothing of these hopes seemed to have materialized. People lived and died and, at best, life was full of mystery, even apparent meaninglessness. And yet now, suddenly, Mary understood that in this imminent birth, somehow not only Israel's history, but all world history, was going to be explained once and for all. All the heartfelt longing of the past, all the waiting, was coming to its end because now, in Jesus, God was at last fulfilling his promise to Abraham, that through his offspring, not just Israel, but *all* the nations of the world would at last know God's ultimate blessing (Genesis 12:1–3).

That seems an extraordinary claim, perhaps even a shocking claim, to our Western, pluralist, multicultural ears today: that in one person, Jesus Christ, Jesus of Nazareth, and in him *alone*, all history should be explained. But this is precisely Mary's claim and the cause for her rejoicing. All the well-known prophecies that we often hear at Christmas carol services, spanning the many centuries of the Old Testament story, come to their focus and fulfilment in Jesus Christ of Nazareth. 'The hopes and fears of all the years'[4] are indeed fulfilled in Bethlehem in his birth. His coming is where the whole history of this world finds meaning: the birth of Jesus explains all of the history of the ancient Jewish people, and therefore all of human history for us too. That is why the Christmas message is still so relevant today.

Does that seem unbelievable to you? Perhaps it does, but consider this: why is it that deep down in their hearts, whatever their beliefs, whatever their background, almost universally human beings sense instinctively that there simply must be *more* to this world, to their lives, to their loves, than what can be explained merely by a materialistic universe? There must be *more* to life than the experience of a restless cycle of ashes to ashes and dust to dust.

Why is it that when we really do allow ourselves to think honestly about the deep questions of life (which we tend to avoid doing, except perhaps in a time of crisis) we find that there is within each one of us what C. S. Lewis called the 'inconsolable longing'?[5] There is an unappeasable, searching desire in our spirit for something more, something better, something greater than the life we experience in this world – a life we feel must be possible just because we *can* imagine it, and yet something unreachable, in that we do not experience it.

Eternity proclaimed by God

This brings us to highlight a second aspect of Mary's song. Not only does she tell us that Jesus explains all of history, she declares that, in the coming of Jesus Christ, eternity is proclaimed by God. Christmas is a message proclaiming a hope that banishes despair, a glorious future for the human race.

The truth is that all decent people find themselves longing instinctively for a better world, a world different from the one that we currently know. Not a world without all the wonderful, beautiful and lovely things, but one without all the other things: the injustices, the horrors, the miseries and perplexities.

But *why* do we long for that? The scientific reductionism of those like Richard Dawkins who want us to believe that the world is explained in its entirety merely by understanding molecules, DNA and genes does not offer an adequate answer, and simply dismisses it as a question that shouldn't be asked! But the fact is, we do ask. Human beings constantly ask many such searching questions of meaning; it is one thing that marks us out from the rest of the animal kingdom.

Once again, I think C. S. Lewis gives us the answer:

If I find in myself a desire which no experience in this world can satisfy, the most probable explanation is that I was made for another world.[6]

That eternal world does exist. According to the Bible, it did exist once in this world, giving us a flash of its light for a brief moment in human history, rather like when you switch on a light bulb and the filament bursts: there's a bright flash of light for a second and then darkness. That is the story of our world. Man's first rebellion plunged us as a race into darkness, and now this dark world is the only world we know. But deep down within us remain hints and memories of the world that once was, because that is the one that we were made for, and in Jesus Christ, God proclaims the certainty that this world will exist again, for ever and ever. Indeed, Mary understands that in the imminent coming of Jesus it is being assured. The total transformation of this world into that other world for which all humanity longs has begun.

> He has shown strength with his arm;
>> he has scattered the proud
>>> in the thoughts of their hearts;
>> he has brought down the mighty from their thrones
>>> and exalted those of humble estate;
>> he has filled the hungry with good things,
>>> and the rich he has sent away empty.

Verses 51–53 speak poetically, nevertheless very plainly, of a transformed world. Notice that the past tense is used. It was common for the biblical prophets to speak in the past tense[7] because the word of God they proclaimed was so certain that it was as though it had already been accomplished the moment God had uttered it. Here Mary is telling forth the word of God just as they did, and proclaiming all these things as good as accomplished already in the coming of her son. In Jesus, the reality of eternity is proclaimed by God to us, the future as it ought to be, the future as we long for it to be: just judgment for the proud, the arrogant and the exploiter, and just recompense for the humble, the hungry and the lowly. He casts down those who are full of themselves and he lifts up those who are empty.

This is not some naive utopian hope, a fantasy about saving the world through politics – do you really trust politicians to change the world? – or economic theory – after the worldwide economic collapse, hardly likely! – or, worse still, through war and conquest, or for that matter through recycling or environmentalism, or whatever else we may pin our hopes on today. To think that we really might be able to make the perfect world ourselves is just fantasy. Human beings might be able to tame nature a little bit, but who can tame the human heart? We only need to look at our television news to see how successful human 'progress' has been at that.

But Mary's words are not expressing some vague hope of making the world a better place by degrees. Her vision is of something far greater: a cosmic transformation. The very last words in her song are 'for ever' (verse 55). What she is describing is eternity invading our history and taking over history. The Christmas message, the Christian message, is nothing less than that. The birth of Jesus is the beginning of that new world.

That is why in Jesus' life and ministry, as recorded in the four Gospels, glimpses of that eternal world can be seen. In his presence, that world's power just keeps breaking into this world's history; it couldn't be hidden when Jesus was personally present. Water turned to the wine of the new kingdom; lame men started leaping; the blind could see; the deaf could hear; even the dead were raised to life – all because the life of the world to come, eternal life, had broken into history for a time in the person of Jesus the Son of God. When we read the Gospels about Jesus, it is like seeing the trailer of a film; it gives us just a taste of the story that is to come, but enough to know that we certainly don't want to miss out on seeing the whole story.

This is the Christmas message. It is not about making the world a little bit better, a little bit more peaceful, a little bit more loving, a little bit more hopeful. No, it is about the birth of a *new* world, a new universe, a transformed universe. It is about an *eternal* world proclaimed to men and women in the person of Jesus Christ, a world where everything will be transformed into the world that we've dreamed of, and still do dream of, with an inconsolable longing. It is perhaps no accident that this longing, this ache in our hearts, so often wells up and becomes most self-consciously real in our experience at Christmas time. What is the greatest cause of sorrow and sadness at Christmas? In so many homes, it is the empty place at the dinner table and grief for the loved one who is no longer there.

Recently a newspaper published some last letters sent home to parents from teenage soldiers killed in Iraq. It was desperately moving to read the words of these young men, far from home, letters they knew would be read only if they died in the field of combat. Just think of those homes at Christmas time, not just that first year, but every year for the rest of their families' lives. Yet even in homes bereaved of those who have lived to a ripe old age, and died having had a good life, there will still be pain and sorrow at the desolation of death which has stolen away that loved one. There are tears, and there is inescapable pain and sorrow even amid the most wonderful memories that we share together. Because death defeats us, always, in *this* world.

But in the coming of Jesus, God proclaims *eternity* to us: a future, a world without any injustice, without any sorrow, without any pain and without death. To borrow the words of Aslan in *The Lion, the Witch and the Wardrobe*,[8] Christmas really is the beginning of death 'working backwards'. In Jesus, God proclaims eternity to our world with a shout of joy. In Jesus, the meaning of all history is explained. There is hope for the future; eternity is proclaimed.

Humanity reclaimed for God

Finally, Mary's song tells us that in Jesus humanity is reclaimed for God. It is not just about the past and the future, but about God drawing people back to himself, reclaiming their lives for ever, even now, through the good news of Jesus Christ. So the gospel message is not just about the world and the cosmos, although it is not about less than that; it is also deeply personal. Right at the very start of her song, Mary is so clear: there is real personal joy for her, already, joy that banishes fear for ever. In verse 49 she exclaims, 'He who is mighty has done great things for *me*.'

Our personal world, too, can be transformed by the message of Christmas. When someone comes to see that Jesus is the Saviour who can forgive sin, who can reverse the tragedy of the human heart and reverse the frailty of the human body, then, like Mary, they too can find joy unspeakable and come to know a peace that is indescribable. They can find it immediately; it is not something they have to wait for. That is why all the Christmas praise is suffused with rejoicing, full of joy:

> Rejoice! Emmanuel shall come to thee . . .
> . . . from depths of hell thy people save,
> and give them victory o'er the grave!
> . . . disperse the gloomy clouds of night,
> and death's dark shadows put to flight.[9]

That is why Christians rejoice and join Mary in her song, singing about their own personal experience:

> *My* soul magnifies the Lord,
>   and my spirit rejoices in God my Saviour.

He is our Saviour too because of Jesus' coming into the world at Christmas. By his coming he has 'looked on the humble estate' of his servants, ordinary people like you and me who are trapped in our mortality under the shadow of death. He has 'looked upon' us with everlasting love, in order to reclaim us by his infinite mercy for our true destiny, a destiny of everlasting joy in his presence. That is why every Christian believer can sing, 'He who is mighty has done great things for me.' For *me*! It really is that personal.

That is why I am writing this book, because God, who is mighty, has done great things for *me*. I want to add my testimony to that of Mary, and I want *you* also to be able to add yours, and join in her joy. It is why all over the world, week by week countless multitudes gather together in churches to listen to God's Word and praise his wonderful name, joining the joy of all those reclaimed for God through the gospel of Jesus Christ. Perhaps that's why, if you are not a Christian, someone has given you this book to read, because they long that you too may come to know what Mary knew.

It is not just that Mary grasped intellectually what joy meant, understanding the meaning of history and the hope of eternity. She entered wholeheartedly into this story herself. This humble peasant girl found herself taken up into God's great story. Because of that, what she said is true: all generations have called her 'blessed' – not because of anything special in her, but because of what God did through her.

Mary and Joseph, and Elizabeth and Zechariah, the shepherds, the wise men and all the disciples – Luke is at pains to tell us that they all entered into this story personally. Nothing could be more wonderful than that, because this story is *the* story, the everlasting story that has invaded our time and our world in the coming of Jesus to answer every inconsolable longing and unappeasable desire of the human heart. The story of Jesus really is the story 'which goes on forever, and in which every chapter is better than the one before',[10] and the message of Christmas is that you can also find a personal place in his story. Luke emphasizes for us the wonder of the Christmas message in that it is not just 'humanity in general' that Jesus came to reclaim for God, but real people, living people, people with names and personal stories, people like you and me. Don't miss those wonderful words Mary utters in verse 50: 'His mercy is for those [that means *all* those] who fear him from generation to generation'; it is for everyone, men and women, boys and girls, old and young, whatever your culture, whatever your background – *everyone* who will 'fear him', everyone who will believe the message that Mary sings about.

Mary's joy came through faith in the good news about Jesus. She believed when the angel brought her the message: 'Let it be to me according to your word' (verse 38). You couldn't find a better definition of what the Bible means by *faith* than Mary's response here to the good news. Faith simply means saying 'yes' to the message of Christmas, the message of Jesus, the only message that can explain human history and proclaim the hope of eternity to mankind, the only message in which God says to people like us, 'I have come to reclaim you, to bring you home to the world that you have yearned for all your life but never seen.'

The message of Christmas really is one great song: God singing to the world, 'Let it be so for you in Jesus Christ my Son.' Mary responded, singing back to God herself, *Yes! Let it be so for me*: 'Let it be to me according to your word'[11] – and she found joy that was both immediate and eternal.

Will you let it be so for you also? For why on earth would you not want to join in this song of everlasting joy?

3

JOY FOR THE HELPLESS

The song of a helpless priest
LUKE 1:57–79

———— ✦ ————

⁵⁷Now the time came for Elizabeth to give birth, and she bore a son. ⁵⁸And her neighbours and relatives heard that the Lord had shown great mercy to her, and they rejoiced with her. ⁵⁹And on the eighth day they came to circumcise the child. And they would have called him Zechariah after his father, ⁶⁰but his mother answered, 'No; he shall be called John.' ⁶¹And they said to her, 'None of your relatives is called by this name.' ⁶²And they made signs to his father, inquiring what he wanted him to be called. ⁶³And he asked for a writing tablet and wrote, 'His name is John.' And they all wondered. ⁶⁴And immediately his mouth was opened and his tongue loosed, and he spoke, blessing God. ⁶⁵And fear came on all their neighbours. And all these things were talked about through all the hill country of Judea, ⁶⁶and all who heard them laid them up in their hearts, saying, 'What then will this child be?' For the hand of the Lord was with him.

⁶⁷And his father Zechariah was filled with the Holy Spirit and prophesied, saying,

⁶⁸'Blessed be the Lord God of Israel,
    for he has visited and redeemed his people
⁶⁹and has raised up a horn of salvation for us
    in the house of his servant David,
⁷⁰as he spoke by the mouth of his
    holy prophets from of old,
⁷¹that we should be saved from our enemies
    and from the hand of all who hate us;
⁷²to show the mercy promised to our fathers
    and to remember his holy covenant,
⁷³the oath that he swore to our father Abraham,
      to grant us
⁷⁴that we, being delivered from the hand of our
      enemies,
might serve him without fear,
⁷⁵in holiness and righteousness before him
    all our days.
⁷⁶And you, child, will be called
    the prophet of the Most High;
for you will go before the Lord to prepare his ways,
⁷⁷to give knowledge of salvation to his people
    in the forgiveness of their sins,
⁷⁸because of the tender mercy of our God,
    whereby the sunrise shall visit us from on high
⁷⁹to give light to those who sit in darkness and
      in the shadow of death,
    to guide our feet into the way of peace.'

✳

We have already listened to the songs of Elizabeth and Mary, who responded immediately to God's word of promise to them. They were just ordinary women, neither of whom had remotely expected to become a mother so suddenly; one of them was far too old, and the other far too young, and indeed a virgin. Yet both of them discovered that they were caught up in something far more wonderful than just the natural joy of motherhood. They were thrust into the saving story of God himself because, as Luke 1:45 tells us in Elizabeth's words, they 'believed that there would be a fulfilment' of everything that God had spoken to them. In other words, they took God seriously, and so they took his word of promise seriously too.

Poor old Zechariah presents something of a contrast. We saw earlier why he ended up in the sad predicament of having been struck dumb for many months: he 'did not believe' that God's words to him would be fulfilled in their time.[1] So he had to learn the hard way to trust God.

For many people, alas, that seems to be the only way to learn. I confess with shame that I have learned much more from God the hard way than any other way. Perhaps sometimes you have been in that place too.

Now, Zechariah was a good and godly man. Luke 1:6 tells us he was a man of genuine faithfulness, a true Israelite walking in God's ways and honouring the Scriptures. But somehow he didn't have quite a big enough view of God. His faith, although real, had become domesticated. He had lost sight of the bigness of God, and the nearness of God, and so he had lost sight of the sheer size and scope of God's designs on this universe of ours. I suspect Zechariah is far from alone. We ourselves, even though we may well be Christian people with faith, often think that our own story is the real story. God fits into our story, of course he does, but really, often he is nothing more than a supporting actor. We bring him in when we need him, when we've got trouble or requests. Zechariah was a man who believed the doctrine, the message about a God who was going to come and deliver his people ultimately and for ever. The question, though, is whether he really did expect anything actually ever to happen. Did he really expect God to do anything extraordinary in his own life and lifetime?

I am sometimes like that myself, and I wonder if you are too. I believe in the coming of the Lord Jesus Christ to end history, to judge the world, to usher in his kingdom. If you are a Christian believer, then you say every time you recite the Apostles' Creed: 'I believe he shall come to judge the living and the dead.' The question, though, is whether when we say it, we actually expect it. And do we long for it? More importantly, do we live every day as if it really is true?

This is quite a question. You can be very orthodox, very devout, walking blamelessly in all the commands and statutes of the Lord, as Zechariah was – there's no criticism here of Zechariah, for he is a believing man – and yet still apparently miss the big thing, somehow asleep to what God is really doing in this world, the universe and for eternity. Yes, it is possible to be a believer and yet not actually be terribly excited about what God is excited about, and what he wants us to be excited about too.

However, the problem here is that this is sinful. We might find ourselves sympathizing with Zechariah when we read this story, but in fact, through Luke, the Holy Spirit of God is saying to us, 'No, don't sympathize with Zechariah here. I don't want you to be like Zechariah; I want you to look and learn.' So he shows us poor Zechariah being punished by being struck dumb.

Now, this is a perfect judgment for a priest of God like Zechariah, because his whole job involves speaking; as a priest, he is to be continually teaching people God's Word. But you can't teach God's good news so as to excite other people to faith, unless it excites *you* to faith, unless you believe God's promises and are excited by them yourself. So God turns his microphone off. I can tell you that it is very frustrating when you're trying to teach and your microphone suddenly goes off, but that is what God did to Zechariah for many months.

Obviously this treatment worked, because in those months of silence, when he wasn't able to talk or teach, it seems that he *was* able to listen to and learn from God, and to begin to take God's words much, much more seriously again. No doubt he ruminated on many things, and much of that must have worked itself into the song that he was able to give voice to when his tongue was loosed. In response to the public step of faith he took when he named his son John (verse 64), God opened his lips and at last he was able to teach the world all the things God had taught him in those months of silence.

I think we can see into Zechariah's own experience of learning the hard way from what he expresses in his song, the Benedictus. Its two main emphases seem very appropriate: there is a focus on what God *says*, and a focus on what God *does*. Zechariah tells forth that all God's words have been fulfilled; he has learned afresh to trust God to be true to his words, and so not to doubt them, but to take them utterly seriously. And he proclaims that it is God who must, and does, act to save the helpless. His own period of helplessness and inability to speak has enabled him to see that all help for the helpless depends on God, and on him alone. That's how he begins his song:

Blessed be the Lord God of Israel
For he has visited and redeemed his people.

The God of promise has fulfilled his promises, and the God of deliverance has acted to save his people.

Zechariah paints a wonderful picture in this song, that of *a visitation from on high*. In verse 78, he describes it as being like a wonderful sunrise, bringing light into darkness, banishing the fearful shadows of death and bringing instead lasting peace. The depiction is of God turning his face and the light of his countenance upon this world in mercy. This is in the very nature of the God of the Bible. In his famous oration, the evangelist Stephen speaks of the time of ancient Israel's Egyptian slavery, and describes God looking down from heaven and saying, 'I have surely seen the affliction of my people . . . and have heard their groaning, and I have come down to deliver them' (Acts 7:34). Here is an even more wonderful visitation of the light and the warmth of God from on high. The lovely carol 'Silent Night' puts it this way:

> Love is smiling from thy face,
> strikes for us now the hour of grace,
> Saviour, since thou art born.[2]

This is what Christmas means: the smile of God once again upon this world that he created.

I will focus on three things about this visitation from on high that Zechariah describes for us in his song.

A promised visitation

First of all, he tells us quite clearly that this is a promised visitation. The first emphasis is on the prophetic expectation of salvation, which is now being fulfilled in the coming of Jesus the Messiah. Zechariah has learned his lesson, and his message is clear: 'Our God has a plan and he keeps to his plan. He keeps his promises. He comes, a God who visits his people as he has promised to do.'

Luke records for us what Zechariah learned so that we too can grasp it fully. You will recall Luke's purpose in writing, made explicit in the first few verses of his book: so that his readers 'may have certainty concerning the things [they] have been taught' (verse 4). In other words, he is writing so that we might believe and trust God's gospel promises. Again and again, this is the emphasis all through his Gospel. In so many of the accounts Luke records, the issue is about whether people trust, or do not trust, the words God has spoken. It happened to Elizabeth just as it had been promised. It happened to Mary just as the angel had said to her. In chapter 2, in the story of the shepherds and the angels, the shepherds went on their way praising God for all they had heard and seen, just 'as it had been told them' (Luke 2:20).

The very end of Luke's Gospel records the story of the risen Jesus on the road to Emmaus speaking with two confused and baffled disciples who don't seem to understand anything that has happened. The women had told them about the empty tomb and the risen Lord, and this had been corroborated by some of the other disciples: 'Some of those who were with us went to the tomb and found it just as the women had said, but him they did not see' (Luke 24:24). Here Jesus says to them, 'O foolish ones, and slow of heart to believe all that the prophets have spoken!' (24:25).

Here is the risen Lord Jesus Christ, and he is still saying, 'What you need to do is *believe the words that God has spoken.*' Jesus says to them, 'Everything written about me in the Law of Moses and the Prophets and the Psalms must be fulfilled' (24:44). Why? Because God has a plan, and when he makes promises, he keeps them. You can trust him, and so you *must* trust him, because to disbelieve the promise of God is sin, as Zechariah discovered. But in God's mercy, Zechariah's chastisement caused a change in him, so that he learned to trust, and indeed rejoice, in God's promises, and that is why he burst out in song.

Zechariah really did get the message. I want you to see just how he grasped exactly what Jesus would later teach these men on the road to Emmaus, for his song proclaims just what Jesus would teach these two: that Jesus is the fulfilment of all the promises of the Old Testament, the Law and the Prophets and the Psalms.

First, in verse 69, he says that God has at last 'raised up a horn of salvation for us in the house of his servant David', a fulfilment of the Psalms, a book full of expectation, for a messianic King in the house of David. Psalm 18 is just one example: 'The LORD is my rock and my fortress and my deliverer . . . my shield and the horn of my salvation' (Psalm 18:2). Now the Lord who *is* the horn of salvation has raised up a Son in the line of David, the promised King, the Messiah, the One to whom so many of the Psalms look forward. Then, in verse 70, there are the prophets: what God has done has been done 'as he spoke by the mouth of his holy prophets from of old'. Then, in verse 72, we have the fulfilment of the Law of Moses: 'the mercy promised to our fathers . . . his holy covenant, the oath that he swore to our father Abraham'.

He really has got it! Zechariah understands that all the promises of the Psalms, the Prophets and the Law are being fulfilled now in the coming of Jesus.

Our God has a plan, and he keeps his promises, every single one of them, always, without fail, for the world and its future – and his promises for you, for your life and for your place in God's future. That is a great lesson to learn: that really and truly *you can trust God*. You can trust that his Word is true and right, and that what he says is best for your life really is best. You can trust him that his ways and commands are best for our world, for our society and for your personal life. You really can trust him in this. You can rely on this God not to let you down, because he has a plan and a purpose and he keeps his promises. Always. He will never forget about you, not ever.

That is a lesson that we need to learn, and keep on relearning day by day. My problem is that I so often find myself, like Zechariah, only ever able to learn that sort of thing the hard way. Sometimes the Lord has had to take things away from me, just as he did from Zechariah, so that I would learn to trust him, and that has been the only way I have learned to trust him. But that was how, like Zechariah, I too began to learn that God is the God of tender mercy. Isn't this a wonderful phrase in verse 78: 'the tender mercy of our God'? But tender mercy sometimes must work gentle chastisement in us to bring us, like Zechariah, to a place of really trusting him.

Zechariah grasped that Jesus' coming was the long-promised visitation from God, and saw that God was being true to his Word. He rejoiced in God's faithfulness, singing about it, because it was so wonderful he couldn't keep it in!

A powerful visitation

Second, Zechariah is equally clear about what Jesus' coming accomplishes. This is not just a long-promised visitation from heaven to earth, but a mightily powerful visitation.

Zechariah gives us a profound explanation of what God does when he comes. His message is clear: our God has power, and he comes with power to save. He comes 'that we should be saved from our enemies and from the hand of all who hate us' (verse 71). He comes to bring deliverance from bondage for a helpless, oppressed people. Zechariah blessed the Lord God of Israel, for he has 'visited and redeemed his people', he has come as 'a horn of salvation'.

We have to be careful here. We might be tempted to think that Zechariah was thinking primarily about a political deliverance, about a mighty victory over the Roman occupiers, the governors of the land. Sometimes scholars have suggested that. But if we look at verses 73–75, we can see there that this 'deliverance' is something that has been spoken about right back in the time of Abraham.

> The oath that he swore to our father Abraham,
>   to grant us
>   that we, being delivered from the hand of
>   our enemies,

might serve him without fear,
in holiness and righteousness before him
all our days.

This oath which God swore to Abraham was long before the
Romans, indeed long before Babylon, Egypt or any oppressors
overcame God's people. Moreover, the goal of this 'deliverance' is that we might be able to 'serve [God] without fear', to
serve him 'in holiness and righteousness . . . all our days'.
Clearly, the enemies Zechariah is talking about who hold
God's people in bondage are the enemies who make it impossible for us 'to serve him without fear, in holiness and
righteousness'. It is *spiritual* enemies he is talking about here.
But Zechariah declares that in the coming of Jesus, God
himself comes to banish fear, and to banish *all* our enemies.
That is why those words 'fear not' are right at the very heart
of the Christmas message. They are the first words the angel
says to Mary when he comes: 'Fear not, Mary' (1:30, KJV) and
to the shepherds – 'Fear not' (2:10). Here too the message is
clear: no more fear! It is the end of fear. This is another echo
of the great prophetic promises of the past, this time in the
prophet Zephaniah. Zephaniah says that when

> The King of Israel, the LORD, is in your midst;
> you shall never again fear evil.
> On that day it shall be said to Jerusalem:
> 'Fear not, O Zion;
> let not your hands grow weak.
> The LORD your God is in your midst,
> a mighty one who will save.
> (ZEPHANIAH 3:15–17)

He comes with power to save us from all the enemies who
make us fear.

What is the greatest shadow of fear that tyrannizes the people of this world, holding us in bondage, darkening our lives, and about which we are absolutely helpless to do anything at all? Verse 79 of Zechariah's song identifies it clearly: it is 'the darkness . . . the shadow of death'. Death is our great and greatest enemy, the tyrant that robs us of the most precious, dearest things in our life and our world. Nobody can do something more damaging to you than take away the life of your nearest and dearest, the ones you cherish, the ones you love and live for. Death is *the* great enemy of humankind and, as we have already noted, even at Christmas time, in the midst of our rejoicing, death's dark shadow so often tinges joy with sadness as we cannot help thinking of the loved ones who used to sit around that table with us. But in Jesus Christ, says Zechariah, God was visiting our world with power to destroy our enemies, all of them, even the great enemy, death, and to take away our fear, and our bondage to fear, because he dealt with the problem at its source.

Why is death such a great enemy? Why does it have such power to rob and destroy? The Bible answers that 'the sting of death is *sin*' (1 Corinthians 15:56). Human sin is the disaster which underlies the whole issue of death, sin that goes right back to the beginning, to humankind's first rebellion against God. 'In the day you eat of it, you shall surely die,' God said to the man (Genesis 2:17), speaking of the one single thing forbidden in the entirety of God's vast creation. And so it was: in the day when man rebelled against God Almighty, his Creator and Lord, he brought death into the world, death as the bitter wage paid by the oppressive power of sin. Sin entered the world, and as a result, 'death reigned' (Romans 5:14). It is indisputable that death has reigned throughout human history, relentlessly like a tyrant, enslaving us all, because as long as sin is counted against us, death has a hold of us. Human beings are helpless, in bondage to the fear of death. But in Jesus

Christ, God came with the power to destroy our greatest enemy, and to save us from fear for ever. He came

> that . . . he might destroy the one who has the power of death, that is, the devil, and deliver all those who through fear of death were subject to lifelong slavery.
> (HEBREWS 2:14–15)

This is what Zechariah understands, and why he is singing for joy! He knows that God is coming to help the helpless, to give salvation to his people at last 'in the forgiveness of their *sins*' (Luke 1:77). He comes with power over all our enemies to destroy death *and the causes of death* – to destroy at its root the dark power of sin:

> He has delivered us from the domain of darkness and transferred us into the kingdom of his beloved Son, in whom we have *redemption* [deliverance], the *forgiveness of sins*.
> (COLOSSIANS 1:13–14)

He came with power to bring salvation, deliverance from all enemies, because he came with power to bring everlasting forgiveness for sins. This is the wonder of Christmas: the tender mercy of our God is revealed, releasing captives from their sin.

Zechariah sees this for what it truly is: a new sunrise for our world 'whereby the sunrise shall visit us from on high' (verse 78). Again, he is picking up the prophetic word, this time from Malachi, the very last of all the prophets of the Old Testament, and the one who had spoken explicitly about another 'Elijah' figure who would come before the great Day of the Lord arrived, which Jesus himself said was fulfilled in John the Baptist. Malachi had prophesied about the day of God's coming, saying, 'for you who fear my name, *the sun of right-eousness shall rise* with healing in its wings' (Malachi 4:2), and here in his song Zechariah is saying, 'Yes, I've seen it! This day *is* dawning, the sunrise has visited us from on high "to give light to those who sit in darkness and in the shadow of death".' It is just as the prophet Isaiah had likewise foreseen:

> The people who walked in darkness
> > have seen a great light;
> those who dwelt in a land of deep darkness,
> > on them has light shone.
> (ISAIAH 9:2)

Zechariah is singing about a visitation from on high, with power to save. This is what Christmas is all about: a new dawn for the world, for the whole universe. And it *was* just like a sunrise – at first silent, imperceptibly stealing in upon a sleeping world – when that great visitation dawned in the birth of Jesus of Nazareth, a tiny baby born in an outhouse in a small town in Judea: 'How silently, how silently, the wondrous gift is given.' Nevertheless, that birth in Bethlehem was the decisive rising of the sun, the beginning of the climax of all God's plan and purpose for the whole cosmos.

A personal visitation

So Zechariah says the coming of Jesus is like the sunrise of a new day, a new dawn for the whole world. But it's not just for the world 'out there'. He is talking also about the world 'in here', the personal world of each and every human heart. His song about the coming of Jesus sees this great event as a *promised* visitation and a *powerful* visitation. It is both, and more, but perhaps most wonderfully of all, the coming of God in Christ is a *personal* visitation in that it brings a personal experience of the saving work of God into our own hearts.

Our God is not the distant, impersonal, unknowable deity of the other religions of the world. Our God is personal, and he came near, right into our midst, so that we might know him, and the joy of his salvation, personally. Yes, he came with power to save, but he came *with power to save you and me*! God's visitation from on high in Jesus Christ is a personal visitation for all who will receive him, and receive in him the joy of his salvation.

The once-and-for-all visitation from on high, the coming of Christ to banish darkness from the world, is just the beginning of a great and wonderful ongoing outpouring of God's grace from on high. It is the beginning of visitations that happen again and again and again, wherever God sends the Spirit of his Son into the hearts of those who do as Zechariah did, trusting and receiving the good news about Jesus Christ. Luke speaks at the beginning of his Gospel about God visiting the world from on high, but at the very end of the Gospel he tells us of Jesus ascending bodily once again to heaven on high. There, the last thing the risen Jesus says to his disciples is to wait in Jerusalem 'until you are clothed with power from *on high*' (Luke 24:49). They were to wait for *another* glorious visitation when the Spirit of the resurrected and ascended Jesus Christ, the Son of God, would come down again, descending from heaven into their hearts personally.

In the first chapter of Luke's second volume, the Acts of the Apostles, he tells us that this was fulfilled when the Spirit came on the Day of Pentecost, filling the hearts of every believer in the world at that time. From that moment on, the age of God's personal visitation into the lives and hearts of men and women and boys and girls began, and it has never stopped since. In Acts 15, James, the leader of the church in Jerusalem, speaks about how God had visited the Gentiles, just as he had first visited the Jews, 'giving them the Holy Spirit', having 'cleansed their hearts by faith' (Acts 15:8–9). Men, women, boys and girls who were not Israelites by background, and knew nothing at all about the promises of God, now too received a personal visitation from on high as they heard and trusted the message of Jesus. God visited them and brought light into *their* darkness. He guided *their* feet into the paths of peace, taking away from them the dark shadow of the veil of death.

Likewise, the wonderful message of Christmas is that God visits us today, just the same, to impart 'the knowledge of salvation in the forgiveness of sins' in Jesus Christ. Our God comes up close and personal, bringing the sunrise of sunlight and glory right into our lives when we come to know him. The words of the carol are indeed true:

> Where meek souls will receive him still,
> the dear Christ enters in.[3]

God's forgiveness means bringing us into a knowledge of salvation, which is knowledge of our Saviour himself. Salvation is personal; it is knowing our Saviour himself. The words 'know' and 'knowledge' above are deeply personal, meaning real, personal, intimate knowledge, in this case knowledge of God. To know his forgiveness by believing and trusting in his promise to us means to *know him*, to know in your own life, your own heart, the tender mercy of our God whereby the sunrise visits us from on high to give us light, to guide our feet into the paths of peace. When you put your trust in the message of the gospel of Jesus Christ, he visits you, and it's not just a temporary visit, but he stays with you permanently. Where faith receives the gospel word, he imparts the breath of life into us. He gives us the pledge of life, the Holy Spirit in our hearts, so that he will forever after call *us* sons and daughters of the living God.

This, and nothing less than this, is the message of Christmas. It is a promise kept by God from of old, a power worked by

God from on high, but a personal offer held out today to all who will believe, and receive him. It is a personal promise to you that the knowledge of his salvation in the forgiveness of your sins will touch your life and bring into it the sunrise that banishes darkness for ever. To know that, and to know him, is to know the beauty of a sunrise that far eclipses even the most beautiful thing in this world. It is to plunge your life into the light of a glory that is eternal and will never end. It is to banish every darkness, even the great enemy of this world that will ultimately take our bodies away, because he has destroyed the power of death over us and pledged to give us a risen, bodily life with Christ for ever.

Zechariah speaks about the task of his own son, John, to go before God's Saviour, Jesus, and to point people to him. In due course, John did that, faithfully, before Jesus came. But my task, and that of every follower of Jesus today, is exactly the same now that he has come: to point the way to the Saviour. We proclaim that there still is joy for the helpless in the light of Jesus Christ our Saviour. The message of Christmas is both simple and beautiful: God is calling out from heaven and saying, 'Come to the sunrise! Rejoice in the light of my beloved Son, Jesus Christ, and the sun will surely rise in your life, bringing the dawning of a new day that never ends, of a sunset that never comes, of a light that is everlasting.'

Jesus Christ came, as promised, with power to save, and he still comes personally, to men, women, boys and girls who trust his Word and make it their own. My prayer is that you will do just that, so that, like Zechariah, even if you have rejected God's words in the past, you too will rejoice in the light of our Lord Jesus Christ this Christmas.

4
JOY FOR THE HEAVENS

The song of heavenly proclaimers
Luke 2:8–20

━━━━━✦━━━━━

[8]And in the same region there were shepherds out in the field, keeping watch over their flock by night. [9]And an angel of the Lord appeared to them, and the glory of the Lord shone around them, and they were filled with great fear. [10]And the angel said to them, 'Fear not, for behold, I bring you good news of great joy that will be for all the people. [11]For unto you is born this day in the city of David a Saviour, who is Christ the Lord. [12]And this will be a sign for you: you will find a baby wrapped in swaddling cloths and lying in a manger.' [13]And suddenly there was with the angel a multitude of the heavenly host praising God and saying,

[14]'Glory to God in the highest,
    and on earth peace among those
        with whom he is pleased!'

[15]When the angels went away from them into heaven, the shepherds said to one another, 'Let us go over to Bethlehem and see this thing that has happened, which

the Lord has made known to us.' [16]And they went with haste and found Mary and Joseph, and the baby lying in a manger. [17]And when they saw it, they made known the saying that had been told them concerning this child. [18]And all who heard it wondered at what the shepherds told them. [19]But Mary treasured up all these things, pondering them in her heart. [20]And the shepherds returned, glorifying and praising God for all they had heard and seen, as it had been told them.

———————✦———————

Angels are such a familiar part of our Christmas decorations and cards that it is actually quite hard for us to read the Bible's account of angels without being completely confused and misled. I looked up the words 'Christmas' and 'angels' together on Google, and almost all of the top hits consisted of images of fairy-like cherubs playing pipes of peace and harps, a picture of absolute innocence and sentimentality. In fact, however, the picture the Bible gives us of real angels is very different indeed. When we read about the multitude of the 'heavenly host', these words actually mean the 'heavenly armies', an awesome and terrifying host of celestial soldiers. That is what the shepherds saw (Luke 2:13), which explains why they were not saying, 'Oh, isn't that pretty?', but rather collapsing in terror, filled with 'sudden dread', as one carol puts it. Grown men (especially hardened shepherds well used to fighting off wild animals and rustlers) aren't usually afraid of cherubic fairies with harps and pipes of peace, but they are understandably afraid of an army of overwhelming force appearing right in front of them – just ask any of the poor people facing the onslaught of jihadist militants in the Middle East at the time of writing.

This confusion about angels illustrates the vast gulf between many popular contemporary ideas about Christmas and what the Christmas story in the Bible is actually all about. We tend to call Christmas 'the season of peace and goodwill', but we know deep down that really that is all just make-believe. We try to create a feeling of 'peace and goodwill', and we can manage it to an extent and for a little while, perhaps as we are decorating the Christmas tree with the children, or watching the twinkling lights and candles or, best of all, if we wake up to that elusive seasonal crowning glory, fresh snow on Christmas morning itself! In spite of this, however, we know that, at best, such a seasonal enchantment is fleeting; it evaporates very quickly indeed.

We all know the story from the trenches on the Western Front during the First World War where, on Christmas Day, the guns fell silent and the soldiers of both Britain and Germany came out and ate and drank and even played football together. It really did seem then as though all of a sudden the pipes of peace were playing, but of course we know it was just that: a pipe dream. The very next day they were back at it, blowing each other's brains out.

It is often not entirely unlike that at a family Christmas today! Many are lucky to get to Boxing Day with any semblance of peace and goodwill remaining: the over-tired kids are bashing each other over the head with their new toys, the in-laws have fallen out with the out-laws, and absolute chaos is breaking loose!

More seriously, though, isn't that just a microcosm of what our world is really like? Peace in international relationships has proven to be far more elusive than something that can be whipped up with wistful feelings and a few songs. This is just as true in human relationships too. We can't turn a sham into reality at Christmas just with a bit of make-believe. You won't save a disastrous marriage with extravagant presents or a kiss under the mistletoe. That is fantasy, and we recognize it as sheer sentimentality to think this way.

The Bible, however, isn't sentimental; not at all, not ever. There is no fantasy in the real Christian message, only truth and stark realism. The Bible faces up to our world as it really is and doesn't ever try to explain it away by playing 'let's pretend'. Instead, it offers a real explanation of our world, one that matches the facts and the experiences of our lives as we know them to be. Our world is not a place of peace and harmony; it is demonstrably not the place that wistful Christmas songs hanker after. It is, in fact, a place of violence and disorder, as we saw earlier. Nor are our lives always filled with joy and gladness; all too often, sadly, they are full of sorrow and fear. This is because, according to the Bible, our world is not as it is meant to be. We have already noted in a previous chapter that deep down human beings sense that our world should be different. That is why we have dreams and fantasies: we *can* imagine something so very different from what we know and experience, so it does exist at least in the conception of our minds and hearts. Yet we also know from experience that the world we live in just can't be other than it is.

This is the basic perplexity that lies at the root of so much of our human angst. It is why we ask the question 'why?' Why must that baby, so innocent and beautiful and beloved, have leukaemia? Why must this loved one of mine have a tumour? Why is that life with so much to offer suddenly cut short? Why so much hatred and war and lack of peace? *Why* are there all these things?

When we ask that question, the Bible doesn't say, 'Let's play let's pretend!'; 'Let's bury our heads in the sand and pretend that this world is a better place than it really is.' Some philosophies and religions try to do this, seeking 'enlightenment' in what really is just taking refuge in unreality and denial. But not Christianity. The Bible tells it like it is: this world *is* a mess! But it also offers the explanation: our world is as it is because we are in a long-running ongoing civil war. We know what a tragic mess a civil war is, because we see it in our newspapers every day as we read, for example, about countries in the Middle East being torn apart by conflict. According to the Bible, this whole world is in a civil war against its Maker, for we have rebelled against God and tried to banish him from his world and our lives. In doing so, we have shut out the glory of God from our human world. The apostle Paul puts it like this:

> Although they knew God, they did not honour him as God or give thanks to him, but they became futile in their thinking, and their foolish hearts were darkened. (ROMANS 1:21)

This is our world's basic problem: we have shut God out, and so he has turned his benevolent face away from us and from our world. Paul goes on:

> Therefore God gave them up in the lusts of their hearts to impurity . . . God gave them up to dishonourable passions . . . God gave them up to a debased mind. (ROMANS 1:24–28)

And so, he says, we inhabit a world that is

> filled with all manner of unrighteousness, evil, covetousness, malice. They are full of envy, murder, strife, deceit, maliciousness. They are gossips, slanderers, haters of God, insolent, haughty, boastful, inventors of evil, disobedient to parents, foolish, faithless, heartless, ruthless. (ROMANS 1:29–31)

Not much sentimental fantasy there! This is pretty much a description of the behaviour that fills our daily newspapers:

the symptoms of disordered relationships on the personal, national and international levels. All of this is a result of a disordered, damaged relationship with God our Maker, the Sovereign Lord of this world, who has judged the world of proud humankind by giving them – ironically – exactly what they wanted. He 'gave them up' to their own vanity and self-rule. So this is the world we proud human beings have made. We are the ones responsible. Moreover, says Christ's apostle, we are the ones 'without excuse' (Romans 1:20), for we have done a thorough job of wrecking all the relationships in this world: relationships between ourselves on every level and (as we seem to be recognizing more and more) between ourselves and our environment.

Of course, we can wreck it – we have shown our great power in doing this – but we can't fix it. Only an act of God, a divine intervention to restore the primary problem of our wrecked relationship with God himself could begin to set this world to rights. But according to the angels, the vast army of heavenly singers, that is exactly what has happened in the coming of Jesus. The news of his birth is 'good news of great joy': the end of fear and the beginning of joy for all who will receive it.

Jesus' birth was an event on earth that passed virtually unnoticed; it was hidden, unobtrusive and misunderstood. Yet, in total contrast, it set the whole of the heavens ablaze with singing. Isn't that extraordinary? Let's look a little closer at the angels' song.

Real rejoicing in heaven

Above all, it was all about real rejoicing in heaven. First and foremost, it proclaimed a message of 'glory to God in the highest' (verse 14). At last God has intervened to bring himself back into the centre of his world. He has done it so that once again, and for ever, he will have the pre-eminence – the glory – in all things.

First and foremost, the Christmas message, indeed the whole Christian message, is about God. It is about God himself being vindicated in the eyes of earth and heaven, and being seen to be the God of glory that he really is.

It is important to realize this because many mistakenly think that the Christian message is really all about people. Perhaps you too think that. Critics often say, 'The Christian faith is just a crutch to help feeble people prop up all their psychological deficiencies.' Sadly, many Christians seem to think in a rather similar way: God is principally there to bring fulfilment to my life. 'My faith is very important to me because I know God is here to answer my prayers, to give me what I need, to fulfil my life.' I'm afraid that this just treats God like a big Santa Claus in the sky, one whose job it is to give you the things you want to make your life better. If you are not a Christian, and this is your idea of what Christianity is all about, then it would be hard to blame you, given the confused message many of us Christians seem to emit. But let me assure you that this is not the Christian message at all.

The Christian message is all about God himself acting to take centre stage in his world, a world that rejected him and, far more importantly, one he himself had distanced himself from because of humankind's selfish and destructive rebellion. Christmas is about God coming back to the centre of the stage. This is rather ironic, because Christmas is increasingly a festival from which Jesus Christ seems to be expelled. Remember the Introduction? Out of curiosity I recently looked up 'Christmas' on Google, and all the hits were about Christmas shopping, presents, trees and recipes. I had to scroll a long way down before I found anything about the Christmas message, about Jesus Christ. But notice that the angels' message is not about barracking us and saying, 'You must put God back into Christmas' – not at all. It is quite the reverse. They are proclaiming the fact that God himself has acted and *put himself back* into the centre of our world. He has done it even if no one else has seen it apart from these shepherds and a few others, and in so doing he has glorified himself *in excelsis*, in the highest and most abundant honour and splendour. All the heavenly hosts can see it, and they are singing about it even if earth sees nothing.

The angels' words are prophetic, speaking of consequences that still await full consummation in the future. When God finally puts himself in his rightful place at the centre of human history for ever, then, and only then, will there be everlasting peace and joy. But the birth of Jesus signals with absolute certainty that the peace and joy we can all imagine, and for which we long, shall ultimately be fulfilled in this world, for ever. The question is, how?

Real reconciliation on earth

The answer is that there is real rejoicing in heaven because, in Jesus Christ, there is at last real reconciliation on earth.

This warrior army of angels proclaim peace on earth among those with whom God is well pleased (Luke 2:14). This is nothing to do with the bonhomie that people try to conjure up at Christmas with mince pies and mulled wine. Rather, it is the real and lasting peace that follows when once again God has his rightful place in the world, and among its people, as Lord of everything.

Since all human beings are estranged from God through their rebellion against God, as we saw earlier, clearly peace can only be restored after there has been a complete recon-ciliation. And we all know just how hard true reconciliation is, for example, in the face of real crime and injustice. The need for justice can't just be airbrushed out of court; we can't just play 'let's pretend nothing has happened' if we have been robbed, lied to, cheated on in a love relationship, or if we have been the victim of violence. Of course not, for there is a cost to reconciliation, and a very significant cost at that. If you have ever really had to forgive someone, you will know how terribly costly that was for you. Or perhaps you know how costly it is precisely because there is someone you *haven't* ever been able to forgive and be reconciled with; it has seemed quite impossible because you have been so badly wronged.

God is the wronged party in the ultimate broken relationship. In every way he has been wronged by us, yet the message of the gospel is that he himself became the great reconciler. He was the one who had to, and did, pay the cost, desperate and deep as it was, of reconciling himself to us. That is why the angels sing about 'good news of great joy': 'Unto you is born this day . . . a *Saviour* who is Christ the Lord' (2:11).

God himself is the answer to all the promises down the ages that his anger and judgment, which meant he must turn his face away from rebellious human beings, would not last for ever. Through Isaiah the prophet hundreds of years before Christ's birth, God had said,

> 'For a brief moment I deserted you,
>   but with great compassion I will gather you.
> In overflowing anger for a moment
>   I hid my face from you,
> but with everlasting love I will have compassion
>   on you,'
>   says the LORD, your Redeemer.
> (ISAIAH 54:7–8)

Only a God of boundless, everlasting love and compassion would do this. But only a God of limitless power and might *could* be such a Saviour. The prophets emphasized that again and again:

I, I am the LORD,
and besides me there is no saviour.
(ISAIAH 43:11)

And there is no other god besides me,
a righteous God and a Saviour;
there is none besides me.
(ISAIAH 45:21)

So only God himself could possibly be man's Saviour. However, at the same time, the prophetic Scriptures had also promised a *man* – a King, the Messiah (the Christ) – who would come at last as the champion of God's people, to restore the glory of God's kingdom in this world, and usher in a whole new world order. But now, in this angel's announcement, what we are being told is that the world will see both of these things coming together in Jesus Christ of Nazareth. The promised Messiah, the Christ, the anointed Deliverer, is himself God the Saviour. He is 'a Saviour', says the angel (and only God himself can save from sin), and he is 'Christ the Lord', the promised Messiah (Luke 2:11).

He – the God-Man Messiah – comes at last, as promised, to restore all things: to bring everlasting 'peace on earth' through a true reconciliation between God and man which can only come from the Saviour God himself, the great Reconciler. He comes, in the person of Jesus of Nazareth, into a hostile, rebellious world, to bring peace and real reconciliation on earth. And yes, there was a price, a very great price: he made peace, the apostle Paul tells us, 'by the blood of his cross' (Colossians 1:20).

No wonder the angels are singing, 'Glory to God in the highest'; even they are marvelling at what God is doing! This heavenly army of angels looks on in wonderment at what is happening on the earth, and it seems barely believable because, as Paul reminds us, it was 'while we were *enemies* we were reconciled to God by the death of his Son' (Romans 5:10). Nothing less than this was involved. It was a real and costly eternal reconciliation between humankind and God through One who was born to save by the reconciling blood of his own death on a cross. There he would bear his people's sins away, taking all the cost of forgiveness on himself, and there they would be reconciled at last to God.

This is why this message of the angels cannot ever be ignored. It was not just a happening long ago in history; it is the 'good news' (verse 10) of God's glorious intervention, in history for eternity, which touches all people. This message therefore confronts the world today, just as it confronted those shepherds 2,000 years ago, and demands a response in just the same way. The rejoicing of the angels was real because the reconciliation on earth through Jesus Christ was real and costly and wonderful. And because that is so, this message demands a response in time that is real.

Real response in time

A real response in time and history is commanded from every human being. Notice that the angels are not vague and general or sentimental about the peace they are singing about. There is no peace for those who refuse peace, for example. Real peace can be offered freely and wonderfully, but it must be accepted and received. There is no such thing as reconciliation in theory, is there? For reconciliation to be real means re-entry into a relationship that was broken and damaged; it means that relationship being restored and repaired and renewed. Reconciliation always involves two sides. So it is with God's peace. God is gracious and merciful, but he is not soft and sentimental, nor is he unjustly indiscriminate. It is those who believe and respond humbly to the divine offer of peace in Jesus Christ the Son of God whose world is set to rights, and who are thereby reconciled to God and know the joy and peace he alone gives. It is peace, says the angel, upon 'those with whom he is pleased' (verse 14) – not because they deserve it more than others, nor because they have earned it, but just because they have heard the message and have *responded*; they have received God's peace. This is what the Bible means by *faith*: responding rightly to God's extraordinary and merciful offer of eternal reconciliation through Jesus Christ. 'Without faith it is impossible to please him [God]' (Hebrews 11:6).

This is why the message of Christmas calls for a response – always, from every human being, including you and me. It can't be any other way, because the gospel is all about a real relationship with God, and no real relationship can be merely one-sided. You can show and offer love all you like, but unless that love is received, there's no shared love and no real relationship. So the Christmas message of God's love calls for a personal and an urgent response: a response before it is too late. I said that the angels' words were prophetic, and indeed that is true. The peace and joy will be universal one day, among all the people of this world, who will 'inherit the earth' (Matthew 5:5) when Jesus Christ returns to reign for ever. On that day he will establish his cosmic peace by force, on the throne from which he will judge and rule this world for ever. As the prophet says,

> He shall judge between the nations . . .
> and they shall beat their swords into ploughshares,
>   and their spears into pruning-hooks;
> nation shall not lift up sword against nation,
>   neither shall they learn war any more.
> (ISAIAH 2:4)

That day *is* coming, and it may be nearer than any of us think. But we need to understand that on that day there will be no choices left. As Jesus himself tells us, those who have not received his offer of peace now will be swept away for ever as in a flood (Matthew 24:39).

'Now,' the Bible tells us, 'is the favourable time . . . now is the day of salvation' (2 Corinthians 6:2). Today is the day to hear the message and be reconciled to God, because when *that* day comes, the issues will have been decided for ever. This is the reason why Luke records all these things for us in his Gospel. He is saying to us, 'Look at the shepherds, and do as they did. They got it right!' Do you see how he highlights for us aspects of their response which he wants all his readers to emulate?

First, they came *personally* (Luke 2:15): 'Let *us* go,' they said. They were humble enough to realize that they needed what the angels were talking about: the peace of God brought by the Saviour of God. Sadly, this is often a big stumbling block to finding reconciliation with God through Jesus Christ. Many are too proud to think that they themselves really need what the angels are talking about. But you must be humble enough to come personally to Jesus Christ; there is no other way to receive reconciliation with God except through submission to the good news of his Son, the only Saviour.

They also came *urgently*: 'They went with haste' (Luke 2:16). They didn't put off their personal investigation of Jesus Christ until a more convenient time. That too can be a big stumbling block for many today. 'There's plenty of time to think about these things in the future,' they will say. But, as Jesus himself warns us in a story that Luke records in chapter 12 of his Gospel, none of us knows how much time God has given us, or is going to give us. To a man who thought he had plenty of time to sort out his life, once he had given time and energy to his business interests and financial security, God said, 'Fool! This night your soul is required of you' (Luke 12:20).

I shall never forget one year when on the day before Christmas Eve I buried a student who was just nineteen years old. Three days previously he had been fit and well and laughing and joking with his friends, but by Christmas Eve we had put him eight feet down into the cold earth.

So you need to come personally: humbly, not proudly. You need to come urgently: promptly, not procrastinating. You need to make a real response in time to the message about Jesus Christ. That is Luke's clear and unequivocal message.

I hope you have already done as these shepherds did: responded really and truly to the message of Jesus. But if you haven't, this Christmas is a great time to do just that. The angels bring to all of us a message full of 'good news of great joy'. Why would anyone want to reject that? Why would you not receive it?

Receive it, and you also, like the shepherds, will go on life's way rejoicing, glorifying and praising God, because you will likewise discover what they discovered: that everything about Jesus Christ is just exactly 'as it has been told' by the angels (Luke 2:20). There's no fantasy, no let's pretend with the God of the Bible.

Won't you join the joy of heaven this Christmas?

5

JOY FOR THE HOPEFUL

The song of the hopeful pensioners
LUKE 2:22–38

———————✦———————

²²And when the time came for their purification according to the Law of Moses, they brought him up to Jerusalem to present him to the Lord ²³(as it is written in the Law of the Lord, 'Every male who first opens the womb shall be called holy to the Lord') ²⁴and to offer a sacrifice according to what is said in the Law of the Lord, 'a pair of turtledoves, or two young pigeons'. ²⁵Now there was a man in Jerusalem, whose name was Simeon, and this man was righteous and devout, waiting for the consolation of Israel, and the Holy Spirit was upon him. ²⁶And it had been revealed to him by the Holy Spirit that he would not see death before he had seen the Lord's Christ. ²⁷And he came in the Spirit into the temple, and when the parents brought in the child Jesus, to do for him according to the custom of the Law, ²⁸he took him up in his arms and blessed God and said,

> ²⁹'Lord, now you are letting your servant depart
>   in peace,
>   according to your word;

³⁰for my eyes have seen your salvation
  ³¹that you have prepared in the presence
      of all peoples,
³²a light for revelation to the Gentiles,
      and for glory to your people Israel.'

³³And his father and his mother marvelled at what was said about him. ³⁴And Simeon blessed them and said to Mary his mother, 'Behold, this child is appointed for the fall and rising of many in Israel, and for a sign that is opposed ³⁵(and a sword will pierce through your own soul also), so that thoughts from many hearts may be revealed.'

³⁶And there was a prophetess, Anna, the daughter of Phanuel, of the tribe of Asher. She was advanced in years, having lived with her husband seven years from when she was a virgin, ³⁷and then as a widow until she was eighty-four. She did not depart from the temple, worshipping with fasting and prayer night and day. ³⁸And coming up at that very hour she began to give thanks to God and to speak of him to all who were waiting for the redemption of Jerusalem.

The first Christmas songs in Luke's Gospel are quite an eclectic mix. The first two are from a pair of pregnant women: Elizabeth, who never expected to be pregnant since she was very old (midwives today call a woman over thirty-four years of age expecting a first baby an 'elderly primigravida',[1] and Elizabeth was likely to have been a lot older than that!), and Mary, the engaged girl, who was also very unexpectedly pregnant for quite different reasons. Then there is Zechariah, the dumbstruck priest, the father of John the Baptist who breaks into song after John's birth, followed by a massed choir of angels who sing to the shepherds about the birth of Jesus Christ, the Saviour. Not perhaps the expected line-up for the Christmas hit parade! The fifth and final song that we shall look at involves an equally unlikely duo, Simeon and Anna, whom we meet in the story Luke recounts in Luke 2:22–38.

The famous part of the song goes by the name of the Nunc Dimittis – which (as you'll have worked out) is from the Latin translation of the first few words of the song: 'Now you are letting your servant *depart* in peace.'

Although the Nunc Dimittis is generally thought of as being the song of Simeon, in fact what Luke records is really more of a duet, because into the last verses of this little story chimes the voice of this other person, Anna. So this is a song sung by two people who share at least two things in common.

First of all, they are both very old. We aren't told exactly how old Simeon was, but the implication is that he was very old, near the end of his life. We are told Anna's age: she was *at least* eighty-four. In fact, the text in the original Greek at verse 37 is somewhat ambiguous. It could be that after her marriage of seven years she was actually a widow 'for eighty-four years', rather than 'until she was eighty-four'. Assuming she got married at sixteen and lived for seven years with her husband and then was a widow for eighty-four years, that would make her 107. So she was at least eighty-four, possibly as old as 107, but either way, she was obviously still quite sprightly and in very good voice. So they are both old; this is the song of two elderly pensioners!

Second, we are told these are both people of real faith and hope, that is, true believers in the promises of God. Verse 25 tells us that Simeon was 'righteous and devout', the same sort of language used in Luke 1:6 of Zechariah and Elizabeth. In other words, these were people who were devoted to God's ways and God's commands. But notice what being righteous and devout meant for such people. It meant that they were 'waiting for the consolation of Israel', that is, for the promised salvation of God which the whole of the Law and the Prophets pointed to. It is very important to grasp this properly. The whole of the Old Testament faith was about the promise of God's coming Saviour, and therefore people of true faith were those who were longing in hope for that day, and showing that faith by their godly obedience to God's commands. The hope of their hearts was visible in the obedience of their lives to God and to his commands. That is always the sign of true biblical faith; people of faith live in submission to God and his Word. So this song is the testimony of two elderly believers, both faithful and obedient to God's Word, and both longing for his salvation to be revealed.

This is why verse 25 tells us that the Holy Spirit was upon Simeon. One thing you can't help noticing is that Luke's story is full of the activity of the Holy Spirit.[2] Remember how he tells of the Holy Spirit coming on Mary, causing Jesus to be conceived in her womb (Luke 1:35). And then the Spirit filled John the Baptist while he was still in the womb (Luke 1:15, 44), and the Spirit filled Elizabeth his mother and caused her to sing (Luke 1:41). And then the Holy Spirit came on Zechariah and opened his mouth so that he could express song and praise to God (Luke 1:67). And here we see that the Holy Spirit had spoken to Simeon about Jesus the Saviour, and then the Spirit had led him to Jesus, right into his presence in the temple (Luke 2:26–27). This is always the mark of the Holy Spirit's work. He *speaks* about Jesus, reveals Jesus to the human heart, and thus he *leads* people into a personal encounter with Jesus the Christ.

The Holy Spirit's ministry is to lead people to see and to know 'the Lord's Christ' (verse 26). That is exactly what he did for old Simeon waiting and longing in the temple, and it is what he is still doing today, all over the world. Jesus' family were being guided by the Holy Spirit's words in the Scriptures when they went to the temple to do what the Bible had told them to do (verse 27). Simeon, too, was being guided by God's revelation, and through this, the Holy Spirit was bringing him into the presence of Jesus Christ.

It is still the same today. Whenever people listen to God's Word in Scripture, the Holy Spirit is there, leading them to an encounter with Jesus Christ. That is what Luke demonstrates so graphically in this little story. When the Holy Spirit speaks of Jesus, and leads to Jesus, and reveals Jesus, then people receive him with joy. Simeon took Jesus in his arms and he 'blessed God' (verse 28); he broke into song, praising God, in a song all about receiving Jesus, about what it means to know Jesus.

Together with Anna's help in the last verse, Simeon tells us four things about what it means to receive Jesus personally as God's wonderful Saviour.

A reception of peace

Simeon took Jesus up 'in his arms', and the first thing he tells us about embracing Jesus as your personal Saviour is that it involves a reception of peace:

> Lord, now you are letting your servant depart
>   in peace,
>   according to your word;
> for my eyes have seen your salvation.
> (Luke 2:29–30)

To receive Jesus as Saviour means to be a sharer in the peace of the gospel personally in our hearts. This peace is not in the least vague or sentimental; Simeon speaks of it in very real, tangible and practical ways, in at least two clear senses. First of all, he indicates that it brings an overwhelming *contentment* about our earthly life and our existence. For Simeon, whatever his lack in material terms might have been, whatever bodily lack or deficiency or earthly wants he might have had, for him to see God's salvation by knowing Jesus the Saviour personally, that was enough. There could be no regrets about his life any more. He could depart in peace; he was happy to die. There was an utter contentment about his earthly life.

What a great contrast to most of what we see around us today. Our world is full of discontent, insatiable desires, cravings, wants and needs, never more evident than in the advertising bonanza we experience in the run-up to Christmas every year. Between Christmas services I was once fighting my way through a thronged bookshop, and I spotted a volume entitled *1,001 Things to Do before You Die*. I didn't buy it (I doubt I've got time to do any of them!), but Simeon would have said, 'No! There's only *one* thing you must do – take Jesus in your arms. Then you will discover that is enough; you don't need those thousand other things.' Peace and real contentment about life is what receiving Jesus as your Saviour means.

Second, peace for Simeon was a *total absence of the fear of death*. Did you notice that? – Let me 'depart in peace'. He has no fear of death, and instead can face the grave without any dread at all, because his eyes 'have seen your salvation'. This too is the great peace that belongs to those who have received Jesus as Saviour. That is why we sing:

> Good Christian men, rejoice . . .
> Now ye need not fear the grave . . .
> Jesus Christ was born to save![3]

It is a real joy and a strength to me when I speak to individuals who are facing death, but don't have any fear of the grave because they have taken Jesus in their arms just like Simeon did. An elderly lady who was dying of cancer once said to me just before Christmas as we discussed her funeral, 'I have great peace!' That was Simeon. It was a reception of deep and lasting peace which overcomes even the grave.

A revelation of purpose

Second, embracing Jesus as God's Saviour was for Simeon a revelation of God's purpose:

My eyes have seen your salvation
    that you have prepared in the presence
        of all peoples,
a light for revelation to the Gentiles,
    and for glory to your people Israel.
(LUKE 2:30–32)

To receive Jesus as Saviour means becoming a sharer in the purpose of the gospel of God for the whole world. It is to see that the story of this world finds its meaning and answer in Jesus alone. Jesus Christ brings not just meaning and explanation which gives peace in your own personal world; he brings light and glory to the whole of world history, past, present and future. Simeon was a true believer. He knew that God is God of all the earth, and he knew that God's purpose of salvation was for the whole world, not just for Israel. But now he saw that all of God's saving revelation for the whole world was to be found in the One who had come: in Jesus of Nazareth. He is the salvation revealed 'in the presence of *all* peoples' (verse 31). He is the 'light for revelation' of the one true God for everybody, to Jews and also 'to the Gentiles' – for Middle Eastern Jews and Middle Eastern Arabs today, for Muslims, for Tibetan Buddhists, for Asian animists and for Western secularists.

So many people in our society simply do not see this reality. They think that if there are *any* gods, there are many different gods or, at least, there must be many different ways to the same God. But no. Simeon saw that the one way to the one true God was in *this child*, who was revealing God's light to the entire world: *the* revelation of God, *the* salvation of God. He is the heart, the focus of all of God's purposes for the universe, God's creation. This is something that anybody whom the Holy Spirit has led to know Jesus Christ and receive him personally, like Simeon, immediately understands. Not only does their own life suddenly make sense in Jesus, but the whole world, the whole of history, suddenly makes sense also, finding its meaning and purpose in him. To receive Jesus Christ is to receive a revelation of purpose, and to begin to share in that saving work for this whole cosmos. We recognize the unique and universal Saviour. That is why we sing,

> Hail redemption's happy dawn,
> Sing through all Jerusalem,
> Christ is born in Bethlehem.[4]

We recognize the saving purpose of God in the One who was born Jesus Christ.

A realization of pain

To receive Jesus as Simeon did means we become sharers in the peace of the gospel and we become sharers in the purpose of the gospel. But it also means a realization of pain. To embrace Jesus personally means becoming a sharer in the pain of the gospel too. There is a dark side to Simeon's message, which we see in the words he speaks to Jesus' parents:

> Simeon blessed them and said to Mary his mother, 'Behold, this child is appointed for the fall and rising of many in Israel, and for a sign that is opposed (and a sword will pierce through your own soul also), so that thoughts from many hearts may be revealed.'
> (LUKE 2:34–35)

This is the realization that to be caught up in the story of the Saviour is to be caught up in the disturbance that Jesus and his gospel will always provoke, in our world and in our hearts. It was Jesus himself, the Prince of Peace, who said that in a very real sense he came not 'to bring peace, but a sword' (Matthew 10:34). He means he brings the sword of division; right from the beginning Jesus Christ has been the great divider of people.

Simeon understood that, and he was honest about it. He is telling us that you can't receive and follow Jesus without walking in his way. Jesus himself says this so many times, as he explains that *his* way is the way of the cross. Simeon is recalling here, and alluding to, the words of Isaiah the prophet, who spoke about the coming One. 'He will become a sanctuary', that is, a place of peace, refuge and salvation, said Isaiah, but *also* 'a stone of offence and a rock of stumbling' for many (Isaiah 8:14). You only need to read on through Luke's Gospel to find out just how true that was throughout Jesus' earthly ministry, and it is no less true today.

Any believer who receives Jesus personally as their Saviour discovers this very quickly, because, as verse 35 says, the 'thoughts from many hearts' are 'revealed' when people are confronted with Jesus Christ. He shines his light into hearts, the searching light of his Word, and many – maybe you have been one of them – are offended by the demands he makes. Jesus will dare to criticize our lifestyle, or our loves, or our ambitions, or our own personal autonomy, and dare to demand change. Consequently, Jesus and his message will always be 'a sign that is opposed' (verse 34). This is a pain that no follower of Jesus ever can avoid, not just his earthly parents. A sword pierces the soul of all of those who love Jesus and receive him. Simeon is honest about this, just as the whole Bible is honest and doesn't avoid the reality of true discipleship, that dark side.

Nevertheless, let us end not with sorrow but with joy, with octogenarian (or is it centenarian?) Anna.

A response of praise and proclamation

In verses 36–38, Anna chimes in, reminding us that receiving Jesus leads also, above all, to a response of praise and proclamation:

> A prophetess, Anna . . . coming up at that very hour
> . . . began to give thanks to God and to speak of him
> to all who were waiting for the redemption of
> Jerusalem.

To receive Jesus personally means becoming a sharer in the praise and the proclamation of the gospel. Whether Anna was 86 or 107 years old hardly matters. What does matter is that clearly she was a woman whose life had been focused on God's plan of salvation. She was a truly gospel-hearted woman whose whole life was spent longing for him to come in saving power to his world, and this was what filled her prayers, her thoughts, her deeds, and those of others like her who were 'waiting for the redemption of Jerusalem'. Now, the Bible teaches us that people who have God's desires on their hearts and God's desires filling their prayers are never ever disappointed. Verse 38 says she came up 'at that very hour' when Jesus was brought to the temple. The Holy Spirit had brought her to the place where she found Jesus, and she knew immediately that her prayers had been answered; she had found the Saviour, the Christ of God. Here was the Messiah she had been waiting for, and she entered his story, for ever. She was caught up in the wonderful eternal drama of God's saving purposes of grace.

What did this mean for Anna, the ancient warrior? Well, she threw aside her Zimmer frame and, because her heart had been opened to the Saviour's presence, her lips were opened and she began to sing! Her response was to *praise* God and to *proclaim* him to men and women. She spoke of Jesus 'to all who were waiting for the redemption of Jerusalem' (Luke 2:38). Proclamation of the good news of Jesus is the truest praise. That is what thrills the heart of God the Father: not the sweetness of our song, but its subject – when his Son Jesus is proclaimed and people hear his name and come to bow the knee and worship him as Lord.

Now, I am sure that some of those who were waiting and longing for the Saviour were like Anna, people of the Bible who understood God's plan and purpose. And they knew where to look. But I'm equally sure that there were many others whose longing was much more vague, people who had become dispirited, despairing, having given up hope of life ever getting beyond their mundane, relentless existence. Perhaps most, in their heart of hearts, no longer really expected anything special from God, no intervention in human history, no saving wonders to transform the world for ever.

I suspect that back in the first century it was in many respects very much like our twenty-first-century world today: many people longing in their hearts for something more – something to live for, something to bring real meaning, hope and purpose into their lives – but never really believing that they would find it. But into this kind of world comes Luke's message, in the testimony of Simeon and Anna's song, that in Jesus Christ we *can* find all this and more: peace for our own life and history, and purpose for the whole world and its history.

There will always be pain for those who follow the Lord Jesus, as long as this world rejects him and those who follow him. Luke does not airbrush away the dark side of Christian discipleship either here or throughout the rest of his Gospel. Nevertheless, his readers 'may have certainty' (Luke 1:4), even from these earliest chapters of the story, that those who receive Jesus Christ as Simeon did will always be a people overflowing in praise and proclamation. Like the angels, they too become heralds of the glad tidings of joy, singing of the Saviour to all those who yearn for salvation, whether they are conscious of what they are looking for or not. This is what defines the true people of God, and what defines real praise, as exemplified for us in the wonderful old warrior of the faith, Anna. In the twilight of her days, she is praising God and proclaiming to all who will hear of the One who has come, the One who is the answer, Jesus Christ: the redemption, the meaning, the purpose, the peace, the hope for all of our hearts, and for all of this world.

This is what it means to be truly Christian: to have been led by the Holy Spirit to find Jesus, to receive him, to take him in your arms personally, and come to know him, as old Simeon did in the temple that day, long ago.

Countless people throughout the centuries since, and across the whole world, have done likewise, joining the chorus of praise and proclamation, singing the song of the Saviour with Simeon and Anna, Zechariah and Elizabeth, Mary and with all the host of heaven.

My hope is that your voice is already part of that wonderful refrain. But if not, then it is my prayer that, having listened to the testimony of these the very first songs of Christmas, you may be persuaded that this Christmas is the time for you to do what all these others have done: come to the sunrise, and embrace the Saviour, Jesus Christ, for yourself. I promise that when you do, you also will find the peace and purpose that they found. There will also be pain, because to follow the way of Christ is to walk the way of the cross with him in this world. But above all, there will be praise and proclamation and joy that will be everlasting, without end, for all those who receive Jesus Christ the Saviour as King and Lord.

NOTES

Introduction

1. Glasgow was designated 'European City of Culture' in 1990, following on from Athens, Florence, Amsterdam, Berlin and Paris in previous years. The only other UK city to have held this honour to date is Liverpool.
2. See http://gcampbellmorgan.com/luke5.pdf.

1. Joy for the hearers

1. 'Benedictus' is just the Latin for 'blessed', the first word of Zechariah's song: 'Blessed be the Lord God of Israel' (Luke 1:68).
2. We are told that Elizabeth kept her pregnancy hidden for five months from conception, and it was 'in the sixth month' that the angel appeared to Mary, after which she apparently went immediately to see Elizabeth (1:24–26, 39). So it seems likely that the foetus would have been around the 20–23-week stage at this point, the end of the 24th week marking the beginning of the seventh month. It is sobering to note that this Spirit-filled little one rejoicing in the Lord Jesus would have been within the legal abortion limit in the UK today.

3. I. Howard Marshall, *The Gospel of Luke: A Commentary on the Greek Text* (Paternoster, 1978), p. 80.

4. Ibid., p. 81 (italics mine).

5. Think of Isaac and Jacob, Samson, Samuel and Solomon, for example.

6. See Hebrews 11.

7. See also Hebrews 7:19; 8:6; 10:14, 23–28.

8. See Luke 20:41–44; also Acts 2:34ff.

9. Most English Bibles translate as 'LORD' in capital letters the Hebrew letters YHWH, which is the revealed covenant name of the God of Israel (see Exodus 3:13–16). Pious Jews considered the name too holy to be spoken aloud, and so, when reading the Scriptures, they would substitute *Adonai* – 'My Lord' – for every instance of YHWH, hence the custom still in many Bible translations. Some older translations use a vocalized version of the Hebrew, 'Jehovah', although more likely the pronunciation should be 'Yahweh'.

10. 'Messiah' means 'Anointed One'. Every king of Israel was in that sense a 'messiah', God's anointed king, but all foreshadowed *the* Messiah to come, who would rule on David's throne for ever, and rule over all nations in his glorious kingdom of joy and peace.

11. This is what Jesus teaches his followers to pray for: 'When you pray, say: … Your kingdom come … I tell you, ask, and it will be given to you' (Luke 11:2, 9).

12. Old Latin carol by Heinrich Suso (1295–1366), translated by John M. Neale (1853).

2. Joy for the humble

1. My personal favourite is Bach's *Magnificat*: J. S. Bach, *Magnificat in D major*, BWV 243 in case you want listen to it. (You should!)

2. Luke 1:26–35.

3. Luke 1:45.

4. Line from the carol 'O Little Town of Bethlehem' by Phillips Brooks (1835–1893).

5. C. S. Lewis, *Surprised by Joy* (Collins, 1988), p. 62. This 'inconsolable longing' is a major theme in C. S. Lewis's writing. He is translating the German word *Sehnsucht*: 'the inconsolable longing in the heart for we know not what'. In the preface to the third edition of *The Pilgrim's Regress* he calls it 'That unnameable something, desire for which pierces us like a rapier at the smell of bonfire, the sound of wild ducks flying overhead, the title of *The Well at the World's End*, the opening lines of *Kubla Khan*, the morning cobwebs in late summer, or the noise of falling waves.' In *The Weight of Glory* it is the yearning for 'the scent of a flower we have not found, the echo of the tune we have not heard, news from a country we have never yet visited', and in *The Problem of Pain* he says, 'You have never had it. All the things that have ever deeply possessed your soul have been but hints of it – tantalizing glimpses, promises never quite fulfilled, echoes that died away just as they caught your ear. But if it should really become manifest – if there ever came an echo that did not die away but swelled into the sound itself – you would know it. Beyond all possibility of doubt you would say "Here at last is the thing I was made for." We cannot tell each other about it. It is the secret signature of each soul, the incommunicable and unappeasable want, the things we desired before we met our wives or made our friends or chose our work, and which we shall still desire on our deathbeds, when the mind no longer knows wife or friend or work. While we are, this is. If we lose this, we lose all.' See *A Mind Awake: An Anthology of C. S. Lewis* (Geoffrey Bles, 1968), pp. 22–28.

6. C. S. Lewis, *Mere Christianity* (William Collins, 1985), p. 118.

7. 'The prophetic perfect' is the term sometimes used by scholars to describe this.

8. One of the seven books in The Chronicles of Narnia series by C. S. Lewis.

9. Words from 'O Come, O Come, Emmanuel', original author unknown; translated from Latin by John M. Neal, *Mediaeval Hymns* (1851).

10. C. S. Lewis, *The Last Battle* (HarperCollins, 1996), p. 172, the very last paragraph of the final book in the Narnia stories.

11. Luke 1:38.

3. Joy for the helpless

1. Luke 1:5–25 tells the full story of Zechariah's encounter with the angel Gabriel.

2. 'Silent Night', lyrics by Joseph Mohr (1816).

3. A line from the carol 'O Little Town of Bethlehem' by Philips Brooks (1867).

5. Joy for the hopeful

1. 'Primigravida' means 'first pregnancy'. The modern church may have largely left Latin behind, but medics are still keeping the language alive! (By the way, in case you are ever in a quiz, the difference between 'primigravida' and 'primipara' is that the latter has actually carried a baby to viable gestational age and given birth. My favourite term is 'grand multipara' – a woman who has given birth five or more times!)

2. Luke speaks of the Holy Spirit more than any of the other Gospel writers do, and in Luke and Acts he mentions the Spirit as much as Paul does in all of his letters put together. So Luke is a very significant theologian of the Spirit in the New Testament.

3. Old Latin carol by Heinrich Suso (1295–1366), translated by John M. Neale (1853).

4. Lines from 'See, Amid the Winter's Snow' by Edward Caswall (1814–1878).